# What the BIBLE Really Says

SENATOR
JIM DEMINT

# What the BIBLE Really Says

*About Creation, End Times, Politics, and You*

FIDELIS PUBLISHING®

ISBN: 9781956454901
ISBN (eBook): 9781956454918

*What the Bible Really Says*
About Creation, End Times, Politics, and You



Cover Design by Diana Lawrence
Interior Design by Lisa Parnell
Edited by Lisa Guest



Order at www.faithfultext.com for a significant discount. Email info@fidelispublishing.com to inquire about bulk purchase discounts.

Fidelis Publishing, LLC • Winchester, VA / Nashville, TN • fidelispublishing.com

Manufactured in the United States of America

10 9 8 7 6 5 4 3 2 1

# Table of Contents

# Preface

WE LIVE IN times of great deception. And now, with the advent of artificial intelligence, it will soon be very difficult to differentiate reality from illusion. The potential for global deceptions will be unlimited. Information has never been so abundant and pervasive. Yet truth has never been more elusive. The only thing more astonishing than the deceptions is the willingness of people to believe them.

The source of most of these deceptions is the political sphere where the quest for money and power poisons motives and corrupts behavior. The evil emanating from political players is contagious, infecting our education system, the media, entertainment, businesses, and even the Christian church. It is difficult to find any institution in America that can be trusted to tell us the truth.

The success of Donald Trump and the Republican Party in the 2024 elections encouraged many Christians and created the illusion that the ideological pendulum in America has begun to swing back toward traditional values and sanity. But unless Christians step out from the shadows of our culture and lead a national campaign of repentance and a revival of biblical truth, this political victory will prove only a brief pause in America's descent to destruction.

Americans must know the truth, and there is only one source of truth: the biblical Jesus. People are easily deceived if they are not seeking the truth. Without some healthy distrust, curiosity, and thoughtfulness, we all can fall prey to those who profit from public ignorance. Consider the following examples of present-day deceptions.

## Deception: Climate Change Is Man-Made and Catastrophic

One example of deception originating from the global political sphere is so-called climate change. Millions of people around the world have been convinced man-made carbon dioxide is causing cataclysmic increases in global temperatures. Here in America and prior to Donald Trump's re-election as president, our political leaders had conceded the argument and begun to dismantle our economy and means of prosperity.

President Trump has temporarily reversed this foolishness, but Congress has—so far—failed to make his executive orders permanent through legislation. Fossil fuels—oil, gas, and coal—have been the foundation of America's success and strength since our founding, but many Americans appear ready to sacrifice our country and our future for an obvious lie.

If people were considering climate change claims rationally, every American would know the percent of carbon dioxide in the atmosphere and how much we need to decrease it to avoid catastrophe. The nightly news would have a banner giving us the daily measures of carbon dioxide.

But nothing like this is happening. I've spoken to thousands of people all around the country, and not one person has been able to tell me how much $CO_2$ is in the atmosphere. Sometimes during the Q&A after my speeches, I'll ask audiences to guess. The responses are usually 20 percent, 30 percent, and sometimes 50 percent. It must be a large number to have that much impact on temperatures, right?

Here's the truth. Nitrogen and oxygen make up 99 percent of the atmosphere, and argon makes up almost all the remaining 1 percent. Dozens of trace gases make up less than one-tenth of 1 percent (0.1). Carbon dioxide is one of these trace gases. It makes up .04 percent of the atmosphere, and man-made $CO_2$ comprises less than half of that! So as a fraction, $CO_2$ is 1/2500 of the atmosphere, and man-made $CO_2$ is less than 1/5000 of the atmosphere. And since carbon dioxide is heavier than air, it tends to stay closer to the surface of the earth. It's obvious this gas cannot cover the planet like a blanket and create a global greenhouse.

It is physically and statistically impossible for $CO_2$ to have a measurable impact on global temperatures. Despite all the claims from the scientific community, there are no field studies proving $CO_2$ is the cause of increases in global temperatures. The world's climate is always changing, but man-made carbon dioxide has nothing to do with it. You don't have to be a scientist to figure this out. You just need to ask reasonable questions.

The propaganda surrounding climate change hysteria is largely funded by China and other American adversaries through international agencies, American universities, and special interests who lobby our lawmakers. China has contributed more than $100 million to the international Green Climate Fund[1] and billions to American universities[2] where much of the climate research originates. At the same time China continues to build a new electricity-generating plant powered by coal every week. China is the world's largest polluter, yet one of the largest funders of climate hysteria in other countries! How can Americans be so stupid?

Climate research is tainted by a lot of money and false motives. None of the past projections about global increases in temperatures have been accurate. And when activists tell you how much global temperatures have increased since the 1800s, please ask them how they measured global temperatures in the 1800s. (They didn't!) Even today, measures of global temperatures are imprecise estimates. (For in-depth reading on this subject, I highly recommend the site www.ceres-science.com.)

The climate change campaign has nothing to do with a cleaner environment or lower global temperatures. It is all about political power, economic control, and the promotion of global governance.

## Deception: The COVID Epidemic Is Deadly and Vaccines Are Essential

The COVID pandemic is another good example of mass deception and the willingness of people to believe the unbelievable. First, we now know the virus was likely man-made in China with funding from the United States, but we still can't get a straight answer about how and why the pandemic happened. The virus was initially very dangerous for older people and those with serious health issues, but there was abundant evidence early in the pandemic that the virus was not dangerous to children or healthy adults under sixty-five.

Yet politicians forced schools and businesses to close all around the country. We were required to wear masks that did nothing to stop the spread of the virus. None of these actions made any sense. We essentially shut down the whole world because of a lie.

Then there was the quickly developed COVID vaccine that bypassed all the stringent testing regimens required of other new vaccines. We were told the vaccine would keep us from getting COVID. Then we found out it didn't. We were told it would reduce the severity of the symptoms, but that also wasn't true. The virus had already become much weaker by the time the vaccine was available. We were told the vaccine would reduce the transmission of the virus to others, but that wasn't true either.

Though the deception has continued and it's hard to know anything for sure, evidence suggests the following:

- The vaccine does not reduce your chances of getting COVID. It may actually make you more susceptible to the virus.
- The vaccine does not reduce the severity of the symptoms.
- The vaccine may depress the development of natural immunity, so you may get COVID multiple times in the same year.

- The vaccine does not reduce the transmission of the virus.
- The vaccine has been linked to blood clots which have led to strokes and heart attacks.

So why does the checkout lady at Walgreens still remind me to get my COVID shot? It has nothing to do with good health. It is all about money and power.

## Deception: America Is Systemically Racist

The greatest source of political power for the Democrat Party is the belief America is racist. They don't just claim there are racists in America. They claim there is systemic racism, a system of intentional discrimination against black Americans built into the foundation of our country.

I wrote a whole chapter discrediting racism claims in my book *They're Lying to You*, so I won't overwhelm you here with a litany of facts. The Democrats and the media scan the horizon for events they can twist into examples of racism. They have convinced many Americans that police are racists even though most black "victims" are committing a crime when they're shot by black officers. The claims of racism abound. There is probably not a Republican in office—not even a black Republican—who hasn't been accused of being racist.

Here's the truth. I grew up in South Carolina when segregation was still very real. All the southern states were run by Democrats. The few Republicans who managed to get elected were the ones pushing for integration. When integration finally became law, Democrat governors still blocked the entrance of many schools to keep black children out. But the system of racism began to change as the political consensus in the South shifted toward Republicans.

After I started my consulting business back in the 1980s, I had the opportunity to work with hundreds of companies and organizations. If there had been systemic racism, I would have seen it. In my twenty years in business during the 1980s and 1990s, I never once witnessed intentional racism. In fact, it was the opposite. Many of the companies and organizations implemented systems of reverse discrimination: they readily hired and promoted minorities often at the expense of better qualified white candidates.

I'm not saying there are no racists in America. I'm sure there are, but I haven't met one in years, except for the Democrat politicians who make everything about race. Like other deceptions, claims of racism are about money and power.

## Deception: The Bible Is Flawed and Out of Date

The Bible has been the world's source of truth for more than 1,500 years. But over the last fifty years, it has been subtly and systematically discredited by politicians, academics, the media, the entertainment industry, scientists, and even Christian leaders. This undermining of Scripture is another great deception.

Unfortunately, many Christian leaders have become what the Bible calls "*false prophets*." They have given their authority to the government and the world system. These leaders have abandoned biblical truth, joined with the progressive Democrat Party, and advocated for climate change, COVID mandates, racism (CRT), diversity, equity, and inclusion (DEI), and other forms of social justice. If you doubt what I'm saying, please read Megan Basham's book *Shepherds for Sale*. It's a well-documented presentation of how Christian leaders have sold out to the New World Order.

## Deception: Christians Should Not Be Involved in Politics

Politics is the process of deciding how we live together. It is part of every family, business, church, and government. Involvement in the politics of our government is every Christian's stewardship responsibility. Deciding not to be informed and involved in how our country will be governed is like the lazy servant in the Bible who hid his money under a rock instead of investing it.

The government side of politics has become exceedingly mean and nasty—and much like war. Good people may not want to be a part of it, but God's people must accept our biblical calling as well as our responsibility under the Constitution to make sure our political leaders serve "under God" and "for the people." Since most political issues—welfare, abortion, transgenderism, for instance— are biblical issues, we Christians need to be involved as individuals and corporately as a church.

Both political parties have elements of corruption and evil. The Republicans are mostly guilty of not doing what they promise, which is to govern according to responsible fiscal principles and Judeo-Christian values. Also, Republicans have certainly been accomplices in the reckless spending that has brought our country to the verge of financial collapse.

The Democrat Party, once the party of the poor and working class, has been taken over by radical progressives who openly and aggressively support all the deceptions mentioned above and more. Traditional Democrats hardly recognize what their party has become: a political party that is decidedly anti-American, anti-Bible, and anti-Christian. This is not a partisan observation. I've worked in Washington for over twenty years. The

Democrat Party has changed dramatically and is now a threat to everything we believe as Christians.

I would prefer not to include political commentary in this book, but biblical truth and the political systems around the world are inextricably linked. The persecution and killing of Christians foretold in the Bible have been initiated in the last two centuries by socialists and communist regimes inspired by Karl Marx. Communism and its more subtle predecessor, socialism, have caused the deaths of an estimated 100 million people, the majority of whom were Christians and people of faith. Today, Marxism operates in the United States under the positive-sounding ideology of progressivism. The Democrat Party is now largely controlled by progressives.

The 2024 elections in the US were celebrated by many as a defeat of progressivism, but these celebrations were premature. The ideology and goals of progressivism, socialism, and Marxism have permeated federal and state governments as well as most American institutions. This cancer can only be eradicated if Americans, specifically Christian Americans, become much more engaged in restoring moral standards and cultural norms by standing up for biblical truth.

It's a mistake to think the political power of progressivism (Marxism) is merely a human invention. It is actually a dark and powerful spiritual force. Karl Marx, a devoted Christian early in his life, later renounced his faith and associated himself with demons and Satan.[3] He sought to destroy all the vestiges of faith and morality and replace them with state control. Like progressive Democrats today, Communists seek to achieve equality of outcomes and to destroy religious morality. They turn right and wrong upside down, promoting anti-God policies, sexual perversions, gambling, and drug use. They marginalize people of faith and call religious morality hate.

Progressivism has many wealthy and powerful sponsors around the world, but the spread of progressivism in the US and other western nations is not so much the work of a well-planned conspiracy as it is a natural drift of godless human nature. The retreat of biblical truth and principles from our culture has created a vacuum being filled by all the unbridled tendencies of human nature—*the works of the flesh,* as the Bible calls them:

> Now the works of the flesh are evident: sexual immorality, impurity, sensuality, idolatry, sorcery, enmity, strife, jealousy, fits of anger, rivalries, dissensions, divisions, envy, drunkenness, orgies, and things like these. I warn you, as I warned you before, that those who do such things will not inherit the kingdom of God. (Galatians 5:19–21)

By pushing biblical truth out of our schools, government, and most public institutions, progressive Democrats in America have facilitated all *the works of the flesh* now evident across America and, unfortunately, even in the church. I will have more about politics, progressivism, and biblical truth in chapter 8.

We cannot count on politicians, journalists, educators, scientists, or even pastors to tell us the truth. So . . . whom can you trust to tell you the truth? YOU! Common sense, healthy doubt, careful questioning, and basic research can easily provide clues and red flags that someone is lying to you. Discovering the whole truth is part of a longer journey but there is a credible source you can trust.

The purpose of *What the Bible Really Says* is to restore credibility to this only source of truth in the world and to reconnect the Bible to public and private life in America. Traditional interpretations of the Bible have positioned it against science and rational thinking. But you don't have to put your brain in storage when you open your Bible!

We have abundant evidence this universe has been around for millions, perhaps billions of years. There is also consensus among archaeologists, physicists, biologists, and other scientists that early humans were on Earth tens of thousands, perhaps hundreds of thousands of years ago. But traditional biblical teachings still claim the universe and all life were created by God in six days less than 10,000 years ago.

That's not what the Bible really says. Find out for yourself. And enjoy the journey!

# Introduction

THE BIBLE HAS been the source of truth and the map to salvation for millennia. It is mankind's only hope for real purpose in this life and for eternal life beyond the grave. The Bible is how we know about God's love and the saving grace of Jesus. But today, the Bible has been largely discredited in America and around the world. And, it seems to me, the leaders of the Christian church and adherents of the Christian faith are doing little to defend the truth of the Bible. The evidence of this failure is all around us.

I recently drove across several states including South Carolina, North Carolina, Virginia, and West Virginia. There were hundreds of Christian churches along the way, one on almost every corner. But whatever Judeo-Christian truth people are learning in these churches is not escaping the church walls. Our culture continues to spiral downward into all forms of sexual immorality, pornography, crime, incivility, and widespread godlessness. And many of the people in these churches are either not voting or are voting for politicians who are destroying biblical values in our country. Many pastors have replaced biblical truth with anti-biblical social justice theology. There's an obvious disconnect between the Christian church, politics, and the culture. Why? The goal of this book is to answer this question and reconnect the Bible with the real world.

How will I connect the Bible to real life? First, I will reconcile biblical creation with scientific theories of origins. Second, I will prove how a correct understanding of Revelation reveals how end-time prophecies are unfolding all around us right now. Third, I will explain why God created the physical universe and mankind. Understanding God's motives is key to understanding His plan. Fourth, I will correct the misconceptions of God's sovereignty and the role of God's people in the world. Fifth, I will show how the decline of biblical truth is shaping politics. And I will prove the Bible is true and is, in fact, the only truth.

There have been many great theologians throughout history. I'm not one of them. But this helps me see things in the Bible most experts can't see. New perspectives and innovations rarely come from experts. Before entering politics, I spent twenty-five years as a researcher, analyst, and marketing strategist. My approach to research often produced new perspectives and developed more successful strategies because I always questioned the assumptions experts used to analyze data and formulate conclusions.

Why do we need new assumptions and perspectives on religion and the Bible? Because we've allowed religious tradition to obscure truth, and we are losing the battle between good and evil. Our current approach to evangelism and biblical education is failing:

> The percentage of Americans who believe God created humans in their present form within the past 10,000 years is the lowest in the past four decades, while the share who do not believe God had any role in human evolution is the highest recorded, according to a Gallup poll.[1]

The Bible and biblical truths have been discredited in education, politics, science, entertainment, business, the culture at large, and even in the Christian church. The blame for this failure rests squarely at the feet of pastors and Christian leaders. Why have they failed? A large part of it is cowardice and the fear of being ridiculed and losing congregants. Even worse, some pastors and Christian leaders have sold out to big donations from godless progressives.[2] But even Bible-believing pastors have failed to integrate God's truth into all aspects of our lives.

I'm not trying to start a feud or discredit traditional biblical scholars and pastors. I'm just fed up watching Christian leaders either adopt the teachings of our depraved culture or hide behind their pulpits while teaching a version of biblical truth that is inconsistent with the reality their congregations live in every day.

The result of this disconnect from reality is what psychologists call *cognitive dissonance,* meaning the mental disorientation resulting from holding two conflicting beliefs. In other words, the beliefs you espouse are different from the facts you accept (i.e., God created everything but it all happened by accident through random evolution, or we're all God's children, but only those who accept Christ will go to heaven).

The Bible has become a grab bag where you take the ideas you want and leave the rest. Why does this matter? Because the Bible is either all true, or it's not God's Word. And evidence suggests that most Americans don't really believe the Bible is all true.

The lack of confidence in the Bible has changed everything about the role of the church in our lives and culture. I can confirm as a Christian who served in the US House and Senate for fourteen years—and who still works in Washington—the Christian church has become largely irrelevant to the cultural battles raging across America and the world. In fact, the church has essentially given its moral authority to the government.

Has your pastor or church challenged the government's promotion of homosexuality, same-sex marriage, gender confusion and gender changes for children, drag shows for children, pornography in school libraries, men in women's sports, late-term abortion, welfare without work requirements, open borders and human trafficking, the outlawing of biblical moral teaching, or the prohibition of teaching the Bible's account of creation in our schools? Is your pastor fighting for school choice so children in Christian families can be educated with a Christian worldview? You may think your church shouldn't be involved in politics. Think again. These are biblical issues, and every church should be involved!

The Christian church has failed to integrate eternal truth, Christian living, and stewardship with real life: family, work, education, politics, science, and the culture. Pastors have separated and compartmentalized biblical teachings from widely held beliefs in our culture. The divide between the Bible and reality gets wider every day. Pastors no longer shape the culture. They either conform to the culture or pretend it doesn't exist. This is not acceptable. People's lives and eternities are at stake. Children are being indoctrinated with a godless worldview. We can't save people or our country unless we are willing to engage in the very real battle raging all around us whether we choose to see it or not.

What are the wrong assumptions being made by theologians and Bible teachers? And how would changes in these assumptions make it possible for a Bible-based worldview to be integrated into our lives and culture?

Most of the problems begin with the first few pages of the Bible: the account of creation. A complete analysis of what the Bible really says about creation is provided in chapters 3 and 4, but here are a few examples of traditional assumptions and an alternative perspective:

| ***Traditional Assumptions*** | ***Alternative Interpretation*** |
|---|---|
| • God created Earth and all the universe in six twenty-four-hour days less than 10,000 years ago. | • God created Earth and all the universe millions of years ago over six long periods of time. |
| • God created the first humans, Adam and Eve, on the sixth day as recorded in the first chapter of Genesis. | • God created early mankind during the sixth period of time as recorded in the first chapter of Genesis. |
| • The generations detailed in the Bible after Adam and Eve until the time of Christ reveal that the earth is less than 10,000 years old. | • The creation of the first modern humans—Adam and Eve—occurred thousands of years after the creation of the first humans. |

The alternative assumptions listed above are based on the literal text of the Bible, and they are completely consistent with credible scientific theories of creation. The traditional biblical assumptions of creation, however, are wrong, and they discredit the Bible because they are at odds with what the Bible really says and with widely accepted scientific theories based on evidence, cultural beliefs, and common sense.

Traditional assumptions also obscure what the Bible says about the end times. Most Christians are taught that Revelation is about the time from the ascension of Christ to the end of time when Jesus returns. However, the alternative and objective reading of Revelation reveals that it covers the entire history of the world from beginning to end. This alternative interpretation is a critically important departure from traditional Bible teaching because it confirms my assumptions about creation and provides a better understanding of what will happen before Jesus returns. Here are a few examples of what the Bible really says in Revelation:

| *Traditional Interpretation* | *Alternative Interpretation* |
|---|---|
| • Jesus returns in the end times during the Great Tribulation and establishes His reign on Earth for a thousand years. | • Jesus's reign began in heaven after His resurrection. |
| • After Jesus returns, Satan will be locked in a great abyss for a thousand years. | • Satan was locked in a great abyss for a thousand years after Jesus's resurrection. |
| • After a thousand years, Satan will be released to organize the whole world to fight against Israel. | • Satan was released in about 1000 AD and began to deceive and organize the world against God and His people. |

A different look at Revelation helps us see that prophecies about the end times are already happening all around us. If we recognize the signs of the imminent return of Jesus, we can be better prepared to stand against the lies of Satan already deceiving millions around the world.

*What the Bible Really Says* provides a completely different perspective of the creation and the end times than the traditional interpretation does. This alternative also reveals God's real motives for creating the physical world. Importantly, this book will make it abundantly clear how the Bible, science, politics, education, and the culture can be seamlessly integrated without the compartmentalization that now has Christians living dysfunctional lives because they believe contradictory truths.

"The Bible doesn't need any scientific support. It is our truth!" exclaimed a pastor of a conservative Bible-believing church when I presented him with these ideas. His response reminded me of a college coed in a television news interview who claimed men could have babies. "That's my truth!" was her only defense. The facts didn't matter.

But the pastor above was correct. The Bible doesn't need scientific support. Science needs biblical support. Without the Bible's explanation of creation, science makes ridiculous assumptions and comes to ludicrous conclusions.

When scientists begin their search for truth by assuming there is no God, they must violate the laws of physics, biology, and statistical probability. Scientific theories asserting that a Big Bang spontaneously created all the mass and energy in the universe violate the first law of thermodynamics which says energy cannot be created or destroyed. Biological science completely contradicts the notion that organisms naturally evolve toward more advanced and organized species. And scientific theories asserting that millions of random mutations eventually led to advanced human life is statistically impossible. Scientists have trouble identifying even one positive mutation.

True science is the exploration and observation of God's creation that leads to understanding it. Much of modern science and the scientific method itself began with the belief that everything could be studied and understood because it was created by a God of universal laws and order. Noah J. Efron said as much:

> Today almost all historians agree that Christianity (Catholicism as well as Protestantism) moved many early-modern intellectuals to study nature systematically. Historians have also found that notions borrowed from Christian belief found their ways into scientific discourse, with glorious results.[3]

Despite its Christian origins, science has become adversarial to biblical truth. This separation begins with opposing views of creation which have led to the widely held belief that science has disproved the Bible. This should come as no surprise. Our schools have been teaching there is no God for over fifty years, and only 33 percent of scientists believe in God.[4]

Today, science is often used as part of a political agenda to mislead Americans. This is evident with assertions about man-made global warming, the COVID hysteria, misinformation about the COVID vaccine, gender confusion and gender-affirming care, causes of crime, sexual freedom, and, relative to this discussion, the discrediting of the Bible and a Creator God.

This book will give you very different views of creation and the end of time. It also explores much of what is between these two bookends of history. I will demonstrate how the Bible—correctly interpreted—is all true *and* in perfect alignment with real science.

I have tried to keep my analysis as simple as possible, and you don't need to be an expert on the Bible to understand my conclusions. But for those with in-depth Bible knowledge, you will need to open your minds and challenge your thinking. Many pastors and Bible teachers present the Bible as a series of seemingly unrelated stories, histories, and promises with general themes of God's sovereignty, love, justice, mercy, and salvation. But to capture the big picture—the meaning of the Bible as a whole—we need to connect all the dots from beginning to end.

For example, traditional teaching says Satan will be thrown out of heaven and down to Earth during the final days before Jesus returns. This is not true. Satan was in the Garden of Eden tempting Adam and Eve. If Satan has been operating on Earth since before Adam and Eve, then Revelation is not just about the end times. And the destruction on Earth described in

Revelation when Satan fell may well explain how the perfect Earth after creation was turned into a hellhole filled with Satan's demons even before God created Adam and Eve.

This alternative understanding may also explain the purpose of the Garden of Eden: to protect Adam and Eve from the violent tribes of early humans controlled by Satan. Connecting all these specifics, it is reasonable to theorize the book of Revelation is the history of the physical world, not just the end times. That means the birth of the child described in Revelation is the preincarnate Jesus (the "first"), and He is the reason Satan started the war in heaven—and this is key to understanding our role as Christians in this world.

A few specifics can change whole paradigms and answer such apparent mysteries in the Bible as where did Cain find a wife after he was banished from his home and for whom did he build a city when tradition holds there was no one else on Earth except Adam and Eve. These specifics strongly suggest that tribes of early humans and sons of God (fallen angels in human form) lived around the Garden of Eden. Cain marrying an early human comports with scientific findings that modern man mated with early humans. The whole creation account in Genesis becomes compatible with credible science.

You get the point. Taking an objective look at one fact in the Bible can change your perspective on another part of the Bible. I'm not changing what the Bible says; I'm just discovering what it really says, what it means, and what God wants us to do in response. Let's begin with an outline of the history of the world.

## *Chapter 1*

# The History of the World

### An Outline of Key Periods from Beginning to End from a Biblical and Scientific Perspective

THIS CHAPTER IS an attempt—using the Bible and science—to present in simple chronological order the whole history of the world. I failed to make it simple, but I hope the outline format is easier to follow than a detailed narrative. My mission impossible: there is no plausible explanation of how the universe originated and how life began. Everything is too complex and well-designed to have happened by accident, but it is hard to even imagine an eternally existing being who could create everything in the universe.

It is also hard to imagine why God would create the physical world and all the people in it. If heaven is perfect, why would God create a world filled with evil, suffering, and death?

Many of my conclusions are conjecture, but they are conclusions derived from the process of elimination: sometimes no other conclusion makes sense or fits with other parts of the Bible. We can't expect to understand all the thoughts and plans of an infinite, all-knowing, and all-powerful God, but God gave us the Bible and science to figure it out. The following is an outline of how and why creation happened and what we might expect in the future. I've used an outline to describe the sequential phases of history in the order they likely occurred. Later chapters will explain each phase in more detail.

## 1. Before the Creation of the Physical World

> In the beginning was the Word, and the Word was with God, and the Word was God. He was in the beginning with God. All things were made through him, and without him was not anything made that was made. In him was life, and the life was the light of men. The light shines in the darkness, and the darkness has not overcome it. (John 1:1–5)

An eternal God has always existed in a spiritual or metaphysical dimension. God's voice—or Word—is the force that created the heavens and the earth. He spoke the physical world into existence. God's Word eventually became a physical man: the Person Jesus Christ.

## 2. Why God Created Earth and the Physical Universe

God wants an **eternal physical existence** for Himself and His family of spiritual beings. The physical attributes of five senses combined with the attributes of a spiritual body will create a perfect body and ideal existence for all of God's family. All heavenly beings will pass through the physical world and live for eternity in a body with physical and spiritual characteristics. Some will live with God in the new heaven on a new Earth, and some will be trapped in hell with Satan. All physical beings are images of eternally existing spiritual beings.

God's ultimate purpose is to unite the physical and spiritual worlds in Jesus Christ—to create a new physical and spiritual heaven on a new Earth:

> [God was] making known to us the mystery of his will, according to his purpose, which he set forth in Christ as a plan for the fullness of time, to unite all things in him, things in heaven and things on earth. (Ephesians 1:9–10)

The physical world also provides a way to **separate good from evil**. Satan brought evil to heaven and the spiritual world. There is no death in the spiritual world, and evil cannot be separated from good. The physical world provided a way for God to remove Satan and his angels from heaven and a way to purify heaven from evil. The physical world also provided an eternal prison for Satan and his demons because they are blocked from the new heaven—only beings with the unique physical *and* spiritual blood of Jesus can pass from the physical world to the new heaven.

### 3. The Creation of the Physical Universe

> In the beginning, God created the heavens and the earth. The earth was without form and void, and darkness was over the face of the deep. And the Spirit of God was hovering over the face of the waters. (Genesis 1:1–2)

This period before the first "day" in Genesis likely began millions of years ago. Consistent with science, there were no planets or suns, only particles of mass and water molecules spread throughout the universe. Science says creation happened by accident with a Big Bang (which violates the laws of physics), but the Bible says God created all things (which is the only true scientific conclusion).

## 4. Creation of Light, Planets, Suns, Plant and Animal life, and Early Humans

> These are the generations of the heavens and the earth when they were created, in the day that the LORD God made the earth and the heavens. (Genesis 2:4)

Genesis 1 refers to the creation periods as *days*, but these *days* are described as *generations* in Genesis 2:4, and all the generations of creation are collectively described as *the day*. So it appears *days* refers to long periods of time—especially since the sun was not created until the fourth *day*, and a literal day is one twenty-four-hour rotation of the earth with nights and days determined by the earth's perspective to the sun. It is therefore highly unlikely the *days* in Genesis are twenty-four-hour days.

The chronological order of the creation in Genesis 1 (planets and suns, plants, animals, then humans) is consistent with scientific theories, and the entire act of creation likely took millions of years. Importantly, the account of the creation of humans in Genesis 1 is a description of the creation of early men and women. These early humans were made in the image of God's angels which differentiated them from the animals. Importantly, the account of the creation of early humans in Genesis 1 is different from the account of the creation of Adam and Eve in Genesis 2. Neither early humans nor animals ate meat:

> God said, "Behold, I have given you every plant yielding seed that is on the face of all the earth, and every tree with seed in its fruit. You shall have them for food. And to every beast of the earth and to every bird of the heavens and to everything that creeps on the earth, everything that has the breath of life, I have given every green plant for food." (Genesis 1:29–30)

After the first six periods of creation, God declared everything He created *very good* (Genesis 1:31). The whole world was a tropical paradise with plentiful food growing all around on plants and trees. There was no cultivation of crops (consistent with the scientific theories that early humans were scavengers and did not cultivate crops for food). Importantly, there was no evil in the world, no Satan, and no tree of the knowledge of good and evil.

> God saw everything that he had made, and behold, it was very good. (Genesis 1:31)

## 5. The Period of God's Rest After Creation

> On the seventh day God finished his work that he had done, and he rested on the seventh day from all his work that he had done. So God blessed the seventh day and made it holy, because on it God rested from all his work that he had done in creation. (Genesis 2:2–3)

There was a point in time—long before Adam and Eve—when the initial creation process was finished. Creation was followed by a long period of peace and flourishing on Earth. There was no sin or evil, allowing unity between the physical and the spiritual worlds.

## 6. God Became the First Modern Human, War in Heaven, and Satan Thrown Down to Earth

> A great sign appeared in heaven: a woman clothed with the sun, with the moon under her feet, and on her head a crown of twelve stars. She was pregnant and was crying out in birth pains and the agony of giving birth. (Revelation 12:1–2)

> She gave birth to a male child, one who is to rule all the nations with a rod of iron, but her child was caught up to God and to his throne. (Revelation 12:5)

The woman in these verses represents God's creative power as the mother of modern humans. God's voice and physical creative force—Jesus—became the first modern human long before Adam and Eve. Jesus was the first and will be the last modern human. He was *caught up to God* to protect him from Satan who was one of God's mightiest angels before he became evil. Satan was jealous of this male child who would rule the world as God. Satan rebelled against God, sought to kill His Son, and caused a great war in heaven:

> Another sign appeared in heaven: behold, a great red dragon, with seven heads and ten horns, and on his heads seven diadems. His tail swept down a third of the stars of heaven and cast them to the earth. And the dragon stood before the woman who was about to give birth, so that when she bore her child he might devour it.
>
> Now war arose in heaven, Michael and his angels fighting against the dragon. And the dragon and his angels fought back, but he was defeated, and there was no longer any place for them in heaven. And the great dragon was thrown down, that ancient serpent, who is called the devil and Satan, the deceiver of the whole world—he was thrown down to the

> earth, and his angels were thrown down with him. (Revelation 12:3–4, 7–9)

Satan and one-third of the angels in heaven fought against Michael and the angels loyal to God. Satan lost the battle and was thrown out of heaven down to Earth along with his fallen angels. Satan pursued the woman who fled to a protected place prepared by God (which may represent the Garden of Eden) where Satan continued to pursue the offspring of the woman:

> When the dragon saw that he had been thrown down to the earth, he pursued the woman who had given birth to the male child. But the woman was given the two wings of the great eagle so that she might fly from the serpent into the wilderness, to the place where she is to be nourished for a time, and times, and half a time. (Revelation 12:13–14)

## 7. Paradise Destroyed and Earth Filled with Evil

The removal of Satan and his fallen angels restored purity and peace in heaven but created havoc and destruction on Earth:

> I [the apostle John] heard a loud voice in heaven, saying, "Now the salvation and the power and the kingdom of our God and

> the authority of his Christ have come, for the accuser of our brothers has been thrown down, who accuses them day and night before our God. And they have conquered him by the blood of the Lamb and by the word of their testimony, for they loved not their lives even unto death. Therefore, rejoice, O heavens and you who dwell in them! But woe to you, O earth and sea, for the devil has come down to you in great wrath, because he knows that his time is short!" (Revelation 12:10–12)

Satan's collision with the physical world (described in Revelation 9:1 as a *star fallen from heaven*) destroyed the perfect environment God created for early humans and animals. This event is described in the Revelation accounts of the first five trumpets (8:6–9:11).

Darkness, death, and evil filled the world for hundreds, perhaps thousands of years. This is when the dinosaurs and other prehistoric animals became extinct. Humans who survived deteriorated for lack of sun and nutrition. Many lived in caves. An ice age ensued. Satan's demons—called *sons of God* in Genesis—took human form and became kings and tyrants. Earth was filled with violence.

Note: We know Satan was thrown down to Earth *after* the creation account described in Genesis 1 because God said everything He made was "very good." We also know Satan was thrown down to Earth *before* Adam and Eve because Satan was in the Garden of Eden.

## 8. The Creation of Modern Humans, the Ancestors of Christ

In preparation for the creation of modern humans—destined to become God's people who would both continue the war against Satan and be the family line of Jesus—God created the Garden of Eden to protect *the man* from the violence and destruction plaguing the whole world. This likely happened between 6,000 and 7,000 years ago. God created *the man* along with the modern animals we know today. Adam—Hebrew for *the man*—was physically and intellectually superior to early humans. Early humans were made in the image of God's angels and given eternal souls, but Adam was likely the physical image of God's highest level of angel. I suspect early humans were connected to the spiritual world without any knowledge of evil until Satan arrived on Earth, But God gave Adam and Eve the choice between good and evil. They chose evil and became separated from God (sin) and the spiritual world.

The Genesis accounts of the creation of early humans and of Adam are clearly different. Early humans did not cultivate crops, but Adam grew crops and ate meat.

> When no bush of the field was yet in the land and no small plant of the field had yet sprung up—for the Lord God had not caused it to rain on the land, and there was no man to work the ground, and a mist was going up from the land and was watering the whole face of the ground— then the Lord God formed the man of dust from the ground and breathed into his nostrils the breath of life, and the man became a living creature. (Genesis 2:5–7)

Adam was created differently than the early humans were. God created him from the dust of the ground and *breathed into his nostrils the breath of life.* Adam cultivated crops, worked the garden, and named all the animals. After weeks, months, or maybe years, God used a rib from Adam to create the woman, the first modern woman we call Eve and the mother of humanity as we know it today.

### 9. Adam and Eve Chose to Have the Knowledge of Good and Evil

As noted before, Satan continued to pursue the progenitors of the line of Christ. Satan tempted Adam and Eve with wisdom and power. God gave Adam and Eve a free will and the option to know both good and evil. They chose to know evil and disobeyed God. This gave Satan a foothold into the souls of all their descendants and essentially made Satan prince of the physical world. When we obey Satan instead of God, we give Satan control of our lives and the world around us. God still has ultimate control of all things but He respects the free will of His people.

God sanctions the battle between good and evil on Earth because it is a continuation of the war in heaven, and God must give His people the freedom to choose between Himself and Satan, between good and evil. Satan challenged God to allow His people to know pain and suffering in this world because Satan believed it would cause God's followers to turn from Him. The verses below from the book of Job reveal Satan's challenge to God, and it applies to all humanity. This passage explains why all humans must go through the great tribulation we call life:

> Have you not put a hedge around him and his house and all that he has, on every side? You have blessed the work of his hands, and his possessions have increased in the land. But stretch out your hand and touch all that he

> has, and he will curse you to your face. (Satan in Job 1:10–11)

### 10. Evil Invaded the Line of Christ

> Now Adam knew Eve his wife, and she conceived and bore Cain, saying, "I have gotten a man with the help of the Lord." And again, she bore his brother Abel. Now Abel was a keeper of sheep, and Cain a worker of the ground. (Genesis 4:1–2)

It is apparent from these verses that after the Fall—after they chose to disobey God—Adam and Eve were cultivating crops and raising sheep for meat, which was not the practice of early humans. It is also evident Satan invaded the line of Christ. We see for the first time that, from birth, some people belong to Satan and some belong to God. The first child of Eve—the first naturally born modern human—belonged to Satan:

> We should not be like Cain, who was of the evil one and murdered his brother. And why did he murder him? Because his own deeds were evil and his brother's righteous. (1 John 3:12)

Satan pursued the offspring of God, leading Cain to kill Abel—much like Satan eventually led Jewish religious leaders to kill Jesus. Satan has been the father of many people throughout history. Jesus told some of the Pharisees their father was the devil. Even Judas, a disciple of Jesus, was a son of Satan. Jesus referred to Judas as the *son of perdition* (John 17:12 KJV), which is the same name given to the Antichrist.

> When [Jesus] had dipped the morsel, he gave it to Judas, the son of Simon Iscariot. Then after he had taken the morsel, Satan entered into him. Jesus said to him, "What you are going to do, do quickly." (John 13:26–27)

## 11. Cain Banished to Live with Violent Humans

God punished Cain by banishing him to live among the corrupt early humans and the fallen angels known as sons of God. Cain feared these savages would kill him but God put a mark on him to frighten any who might consider harming him (we don't know what this mark looked like, but it might have been the mark of the beast mentioned in Revelation). Cain's physical and intellectual superiority made him an instant leader among the inferior humans who were still living as scavengers and savages.

> [The LORD said,] When you work the ground, it shall no longer yield to you its

> strength. You shall be a fugitive and a wanderer on the earth." Cain said to the LORD, "My punishment is greater than I can bear. Behold, you have driven me today away from the ground, and from your face I shall be hidden. I shall be a fugitive and a wanderer on the earth, and whoever finds me will kill me." Then the LORD said to him, "Not so! If anyone kills Cain, vengeance shall be taken on him sevenfold." And the LORD put a mark on Cain, lest any who found him should attack him. Then Cain went away from the presence of the LORD and settled in the land of Nod, east of Eden. (Genesis 4:12–16)

Cain took a wife from among the tribes he joined (science confirms that modern humans mated with early humans). Cain also built a city for the nomadic tribesmen. He and his descendants taught the people to farm, live in homes, forge metal, and make musical instruments.

The daughters of Cain were far more beautiful than the other women of the tribe. Satan's fallen angels who were living as humans took these beautiful women as their wives. The offspring of these unions were mighty men—including giants—who became the powerful and corrupt leaders of the people.

> When man began to multiply on the face of the land and daughters were born to them, the sons of God saw that the daughters of man were attractive. And they took as their wives any they chose. Then the LORD said, "My Spirit shall not abide in man forever, for he is flesh: his days shall be 120 years." The Nephilim were on the earth in those days, and also afterward, when the sons of God came in to the daughters of man and they bore children to them. These were the mighty men who were of old, the men of renown. (Genesis 6:1–4)

## 12. Adam's Lineage of Righteousness and Cain's Lineage of Evil

Adam and Eve had other children, including Seth who worshipped God and was a forefather of Noah whom God called "a righteous man" (Genesis 6:9). Cain's descendants produced violence and evil. God announced He would *blot out man* from the earth, except for Noah.

> The LORD saw that the wickedness of man was great in the earth, and that every intention of the thoughts of his heart was only evil continually. And the LORD regretted

> that he had made man on the earth, and it grieved him to his heart. So the Lord said, "I will blot out man whom I have created from the face of the land, man and animals and creeping things and birds of the heavens, for I am sorry that I have made them." But Noah found favor in the eyes of the Lord. (Genesis 6:5–8)

## 13. God Destroyed the Earth with a Flood But Saved Noah's Family

God decided to destroy the earth and all evil with a great flood. He told Noah to build a very large boat to save himself, his wife, his sons and daughters-in-law, and two of every animal species.

> God said to Noah, "I have determined to make an end of all flesh, for the earth is filled with violence through them. Behold, I will destroy them with the earth. Make yourself an ark of gopher wood." (Genesis 6:13–14)

It took Noah and his sons decades to build this boat that would be larger than a football field. They were certainly the brunt of many jokes for building a boat nowhere near water. But public attitudes toward them likely changed quickly when it began to rain and flood.

> All the fountains of the great deep burst forth, and the windows of the heavens were opened. (Genesis 7:11)

The deluge from the heavens came from the large canopy of water vapor that had been high above the earth since the creation when waters were divided above and below the sky. This canopy of water vapor made the whole earth a greenhouse that had tropical weather from pole to pole.

The weight of the waters falling from the sky likely caused Earth's surface to collapse into the large reservoirs of water hidden deep within the earth and to push fountains of water to the surface. Earth's entire surface was reshaped with large sections collapsing miles below their original positions, leaving higher areas that became our hills and mountains.

Humans, animals, and plants were washed away, and as the waters rushed into drains carrying debris into the earth, this decaying organic material was deposited deep below Earth's surface. There is no other plausible explanation for how large reservoirs of fossil fuels—oil, natural gas, and shale—can be found thousands of feet below the surface of the earth.

Waters also rushed into the deep basins created on Earth's surface when large areas collapsed deep below what is now sea level. This collapse created the large oceans we have today. Floodwaters rushing toward these deep reservoirs eroded soil on their way, creating valleys, canyons, and riverbeds all around the world. When all the waters settled, more than two-thirds of the earth was covered with water.

When Noah's ark came to rest on a mountainside, the whole earth was bare. All evidence of thousands of years of civilizations was washed away and covered with layers of mud and rock. But by the time Noah, his family, and the animals left the ark, vegetation had begun to spring up around the world.

Many of Satan's demons, who took human form, were destroyed in the flood. All the evil people were dead, and the world was made new. Noah and his family still carried their sin nature, but the world was no longer consumed by the evil from the sons of God. Satan, however, was still pursuing the sons of Man, — the line of Jesus Christ.

The Great Flood occurred approximately 4,500 years ago.

## 14. God Created His Physical Family on Earth

The descendants of Noah's sons created many tribes and nations. All the people alive today are descendants of the three sons of Noah. His son Shem was a forefather of Abram who became the patriarch of the Jews, God's physical people on Earth.

Abram (renamed Abraham)—fathered Isaac, who fathered Jacob (whom God renamed Israel), and who was the father of twelve sons whose descendants became the twelve tribes of Israel. God used the nation of Israel to bring the Word of God to all the people of the world and to show His spiritual family what they must endure on Earth: slavery to sin (slavery in Egypt); protection from God's judgment of sin (Passover); redemption and justification (escape from Egypt); freedom not to accept God's grace (Israel decided not to enter the Promised Land); the consequences of disobeying God (forty years in the desert and living under the Law); repenting of sin, accepting Jesus as Savior and Lord, and entering God's rest (crossing the Jordan into the Promised Land); living as God's people on Earth (the rewards of obedience and the consequences of disobedience as the nation of God); God's discipline of His people (the destruction of Israel); and God's final salvation (the Second Coming of Jesus Christ).

Even today, the reconstituted nation of Israel is a sign of the Second Coming of Jesus. God promised to bring His physical people back together in preparation for the final battle between good and evil.

## 15. God Became a Man, Established His Kingdom on Earth, and Defeated Satan and Death

> The Word became flesh and dwelt among us, and we have seen his glory, glory as of the only Son from the Father, full of grace and truth. (John 1:14)

The voice of God that created the physical universe became a human being: Jesus the Messiah (Savior). This same person was the firstborn before the creation of Adam but was taken up to God for protection from Satan until He came to Earth as a child to save His people.

God became a human being to die for the salvation of all His people from sin and death. God took our punishment on Himself and freed His people from slavery to sin. His salvation is free but to know God during their physical lives, people must humble themselves, repent, and accept Jesus as Savior and Lord.

Many of God's people waste their whole lives outside God's kingdom much like a whole generation of Jews died in the desert without ever accepting God's promise. Jesus is always knocking at the door of His people's hearts, but we must open the door:

> Behold, I stand at the door and knock. If anyone hears my voice and opens the door, I

> will come in to him and eat with him, and he with me. (Revelation 3:20)

Jesus's life, death, and resurrection established God's spiritual kingdom on Earth. His twelve disciples were the spiritual counterparts of the twelve tribes of God's physical family. As a Jew with spiritual and physical blood, Jesus united the physical and spiritual family of God. And His Holy Spirit dissolved the barriers between the physical and spiritual worlds. The blood of Jesus—because it is the only blood that is both physical and spiritual—is the only way physical beings can enter the new physical and spiritual heaven:

> Remember that at one time you Gentiles in the flesh, called "the uncircumcision" by what is called the circumcision, which is made in the flesh by hands—remember that you were at that time separated from Christ, alienated from the commonwealth of Israel and strangers to the covenants of promise, having no hope and without God in the world. But now in Christ Jesus you who once were far off have been brought near by the blood of Christ.
> For he himself is our peace, who has made us both one and has broken down in his flesh the dividing wall of hostility by abolishing the law of commandments expressed in ordinances,

> that he might create in himself one new man in place of the two, so making peace, and might reconcile us both to God in one body through the cross, thereby killing the hostility. (Ephesians 2:11–16)

Satan achieved his goal of killing God, but with His resurrection, Jesus defeated Satan and then locked him in a spiritual prison for 1,000 years.

> Then I saw an angel coming down from heaven, holding in his hand the key to the bottomless pit and a great chain. And he seized the dragon, that ancient serpent, who is the devil and Satan, and bound him for a thousand years, and threw him into the pit, and shut it and sealed it over him, so that he might not deceive the nations any longer, until the thousand years were ended. After that he must be released for a little while. (Revelation 20:1–3)

World history revolves around the birth, life, death, and resurrection of Jesus Christ. Calendars for every country, every race, every religion are pegged to the life of Jesus. No other person in history comes close to matching the impact Jesus had and still has on the world.

## 16. The First Thousand Years After the Resurrection of Jesus

> Jesus came and said to [his disciples], "All authority in heaven and on earth has been given to me. Go therefore and make disciples of all nations, baptizing them in the name of the Father and of the Son and of the Holy Spirit, teaching them to observe all that I have commanded you. And behold, I am with you always, to the end of the age". (Matthew 28:18–20)

Jesus's reign began after His resurrection and ascension. He was given all authority in heaven and on Earth. But His authority on Earth was carried out by His followers by the power of the Holy Spirit. Jesus did not control the events on Earth even though He had ultimate authority.

> So then the Lord Jesus, after he had spoken to them, was taken up into heaven and sat down at the right hand of God. (Mark 16:19)

During the first thousand years after Jesus's resurrection, Christianity spread throughout the world and became the dominant religion. The widespread persecution and killing of Christians continued for several hundred years until many countries adopted

Christianity as their official religion. The Roman Empire adopted Christianity as its official religion in 395 AD.

Nation-states began to replace kingdoms, and all of Christianity converged into the Roman Catholic Church. Unfortunately, as the Bible predicted, the church began to weld its power to governments. Kings and tyrants could act with the supposed authority of the church.

For the first thousand years after the life and the resurrection of Jesus, Satan was bound and locked in the bottomless pit, but the sin nature of humans and Satan's demons continued to corrupt the world. During the same period, Jesus was reigning in heaven alongside those who were persecuted and killed for following Him on Earth. These followers were part of the first resurrection. The people on Earth—the children of Satan and the followers of Jesus—were engaged in a constant battle between good and evil. The gospel of Jesus spread throughout the world but the children of Satan were actively fighting against the followers of Jesus even within the Church.

## 17. 1000 AD: Satan Was Released and Began His Campaign of Evil and Deception

When the thousand years are ended, Satan
will be released from his prison and will come

> out to deceive the nations that are at the four corners of the earth, Gog and Magog, to gather them for battle; their number is like the sand of the sea. (Revelation 20:7–8)

The battle between good and evil was raging on Earth for the first 1,000 years after the life of Jesus, but Satan was locked in a prison to allow the gospel to be preached around the world and the Church to grow. But after 1000 years, Satan was released to deceive all the people of the world who are not God's people and to prepare for the final great battle between good and evil.

The presence of Satan on Earth changed the balance in the war between good and evil. In 1009 AD, Muslims destroyed the Holy Sepulcher in Jerusalem, the temporary burial place of Jesus. In 1054 AD, the first great division in the Christian church occurred when the Eastern Orthodox Church separated from the Western Roman Church. In 1073 AD, Gregory VII established a strong papacy and exerted power over English and French kings and German emperors.

In 1095 AD, at the Council of Claremont, Pope Urban II called for a holy war to retake control of Jerusalem from Muslims. This launched the Crusades, an effort to regain control of the Holy Land that lasted 200 years.

The second millennium was characterized by the growth and increasing hostility between the world's two largest religious groups: Christianity and Islam. Jews were banished from the Promised Land, and the city of Jerusalem was largely controlled by Muslims. A mosque had already been built on the Dome of the Rock in 700 AD where the Jewish temple once stood, and Muslim control continued through the second millennium. The prophet Muhammad is said to have ascended to heaven from the place where the Jewish temple once stood.

> Let no one deceive you in any way. For that day will not come, unless the rebellion comes first, and the man of lawlessness is revealed, the son of destruction, who opposes and exalts himself against every so-called god or object of worship, so that he takes his seat in the temple of God, proclaiming himself to be God. (2 Thessalonians 2:3–4)

The second millennium was also characterized by the growing organization and increasing tension between nation-states around the world. There were continuous and increasingly disastrous wars leading up to major world wars in the twentieth century and the first use of nuclear weapons. Marxism and communism resulted in the deaths of millions of people.

Plagues, such as the Black Plague in the fourteenth century, killed up to half of the world's population.

## 18. 2000 AD: Satan Organizing for the Final Battle

> Nation will rise against nation, and kingdom against kingdom. There will be great earthquakes, and in various places famines and pestilences. And there will be terrors and great signs from heaven. But before all this they will lay their hands on you and persecute you, delivering you up to the synagogues and prisons, and you will be brought before kings and governors for my name's sake. (Jesus speaking about the end times in Luke 21:10–12)

The third millennium has begun the countdown for the return of Jesus. The year 2000 was ushered in with great fear of a Y2K bug causing a worldwide computer collapse. The next year on September 11, Muslims attacked the United States, killing thousands and destroying billions of dollars of property. The US responded by invading Afghanistan. In 2002, the European Union created a central currency—the euro—thereby launching the globalist initiative of the world's elite. In 2003, the US led a group of allied nations in the invasion of Iraq.

The creation of Facebook, the iPhone, Twitter, and other social media forever changed global communications by instantly connecting people all around the world. Worldwide connections soon created global vulnerabilities in the financial markets: 2008 saw the collapse of US financial instruments, causing trillions of dollars of losses around the world.

Over a million people around the world have been killed by major earthquakes since 2000, and seismic activity continues to increase. Millions also died from the COVID epidemic.

Signs of the end of time are all around us. The stage is set for the final battle.

## 19. 2020 AD: The Rise of Godlessness, Hate, and Violence Against God's People

The rise of hatred against God's people—Jews and Christians—is another sign of the coming end of time. Anti-Jew and anti-Israel sentiment is being displayed in protests and acts of violence around the world. Those who hold hatred against the Jews also hate Bible-believing Christians and biblical truth.

Satan is using Muslims and traditional Christian churches to deceive the nations. Many Protestant and Catholic leaders are denying biblical truth and promoting godless immorality. These have joined the false prophets of Islam to war against the truth of God's

Word. Collectively, these Antichrists likely represent the second beast and the false prophet in Revelation. These false prophets align their power with governments, giving secular immorality the imprimatur of religion.

## 20. The Destruction of the United States of America and the Rapture of God's People

The United States appears to be the book of Revelation's *great prostitute* and *Babylon* that sit on—that essentially control—the whole world. Russian, China, India, Brazil, and several of the Arab nations (led by Satan, also known as the beast) are already conspiring to challenge the United States and its western allies.[1] As President Trump cuts off massive aid to America's allies, we have found America has few friends unless we allow other countries to pillage our wealth and resources. Our NATO partners are beginning to conspire with America's enemies because President Trump has demanded they pay their fair share of military expenses.

Satan will soon become a charismatic global leader appointed by the nations of the world to destroy the US and Israel.

> The angel said to me [John], "The waters
> that you saw, where the prostitute is seated,

> are peoples and multitudes and nations and languages. And the ten horns that you saw, they and the beast will hate the prostitute. They will make her desolate and naked, and devour her flesh and burn her up with fire, for God has put it into their hearts to carry out his purpose by being of one mind and handing over their royal power to the beast, until the words of God are fulfilled." (Revelation 17:15–17)

The United States has become the most unrighteous nation in world—promoting sexual immorality, godlessness, and idolatrous excesses all around the world. The US produces most of the pornography in the world which leads to the kidnapping of children, the exploitation of women, and the corruption of the human spirit. And, as President Trump's Department of Government Efficiency has found, much of America's foreign aid has been used to promote immorality around the world. We can only hope President Trump will reverse America's role as the world's most powerful promoter of godlessness.

There will soon come a day—and it may have already come—when the rest of the world tires of America's immorality, economic manipulation, and military dominance, especially now that the United States has stopped being the world's biggest sucker. These nations will likely first conspire to destroy the American dollar, using America's massive debt to undermine our currency, wreck our economy, and throw the whole nation into chaos. Hunger, starvation, and violence will consume our nation. Then (I'm guessing here) there will be a nuclear attack on a major city, perhaps New York and other port cities in America. All trade with other nations will cease, and economic activity in America will essentially stop. America is the only nation in the world today that matches the description of Babylon in Revelation:

> Fallen, fallen is Babylon the great!
> She has become a dwelling place for demons,
> a haunt for every unclean spirit,
> a haunt for every unclean bird,
> a haunt for every unclean and detestable beast.
> For all nations have drunk
> the wine of the passion of her sexual immorality,
> and the kings of the earth have committed immorality with her,
> and the merchants of the earth have grown rich from the power of her luxurious living.
> (Revelation 18:2–3)

The whole world will watch as America burns and surrenders unconditionally to the international coalition:

> The merchants of these wares, who gained
> wealth from her, will stand far off, in fear of
> her torment, weeping and mourning aloud,
> "Alas, alas, for the great city
> that was clothed in fine linen,
> in purple and scarlet,
> adorned with gold,
> with jewels, and with pearls!
> For in a single hour all this wealth has been
> laid waste."
> And all shipmasters and seafaring men, sailors
> and all whose trade is on the sea, stood far off
> and cried out as they saw the smoke of her
> burning,
> "What city was like the great city?"
> (Revelation 18:15–18)

The rapture of God's people in America and from all around the world will occur as America descends into its destruction.

> Then I heard another voice from heaven saying,
> "Come out of her, my people,
> lest you take part in her sins,

> lest you share in her plagues;
> for her sins are heaped high as heaven,
> and God has remembered her iniquities".
> (Revelation 18:4–5)

## 21. Jesus Returns and Destroys the Global Coalition As It Attacks Israel

Some Bible scholars believe Jesus provided a timeline for the beginning of the end times when He used a blooming fig leaf as a metaphor for the re-establishment of Israel which happened in 1948. He said the generation after Israel becomes a nation will not pass away until the signs of His return become evident. A generation in the Bible was often forty years, but in Genesis God said the days of mankind would be 120 years, so it's hard to be definitive about the years in a generation. If we use the average life expectancy today of seventy-six years as the measure of a generation, we land in 2024, the year Donald Trump was re-elected president.

> "From the fig tree learn its lesson: as soon as its branch becomes tender and puts out its leaves, you know that summer is near. So also, when you see all these things, you know that he is near, at the very gates. Truly, I say to you, this generation will not pass away until all these things take place. Heaven and earth will

> pass away, but my words will not pass away".
> (Matthew 24:32–35)

It is a mistake to guess the date of the return of Jesus, but God gives us signs—the rise of sexual immorality, wars and rumors of wars, plagues, earthquakes, and global government—to help us determine when the end is near. These signs will increase in frequency much like labor pains before the birth of a child.

After the United States is destroyed and God's people are raptured to heaven, the global coalition of nations will attack Israel from all sides. God will intervene and destroy their armies. Then Satan, who has deceived the nations for over a thousand years, will be thrown into a lake of fire for eternity along with his demons and all the godless people left on Earth:

> When the thousand years are ended, Satan will be released from his prison and will come out to deceive the nations that are at the four corners of the earth, Gog and Magog, to gather them for battle; their number is like the sand of the sea. And they marched up over the broad plain of the earth and surrounded the camp of the saints and the beloved city, but fire came down from heaven and consumed them, and the devil who had deceived them

> was thrown into the lake of fire and sulfur where the beast and the false prophet were, and they will be tormented day and night forever and ever." (Revelation 20:7–10)

Jesus returns while the nations of the world—led by Satan in human form—are attacking Israel.

> Then I saw heaven opened, and behold, a white horse! The one sitting on it is called Faithful and True, and in righteousness he judges and makes war . . . And I saw the beast and the kings of the earth with their armies gathered to make war against him who was sitting on the horse and against his army. And the beast was captured, and with it the false prophet who in its presence had done the signs by which he deceived those who had received the mark of the beast and those who worshiped its image. These two were thrown alive into the lake of fire that burns with sulfur. And the rest were slain by the sword that came from the mouth of him who was sitting on the horse, and all the birds were gorged with their flesh. (Revelation 19:11,19–21)

## 22. Heaven and Earth Are Replaced by an Eternal New Heaven on a New Earth

> Then I saw a new heaven and a new earth, for the first heaven and the first earth had passed away, and the sea was no more. And I saw the holy city, new Jerusalem, coming down out of heaven from God, prepared as a bride adorned for her husband. And I heard a loud voice from the throne saying, "Behold, the dwelling place of God is with man. He will dwell with them, and they will be his people, and God himself will be with them as their God. He will wipe away every tear from their eyes, and death shall be no more, neither shall there be mourning, nor crying, nor pain anymore, for the former things have passed away." (Revelation 21:1–4)

As promised, God unifies heaven and Earth into a new heaven on the new Earth, all under the rule of Jesus Christ. The whole Earth is like a recreated Garden of Eden, and the people have physical and spiritual bodies like the resurrected Jesus. He had human characteristics but could pass through walls, disappear, and transport Himself long distances instantly. And He rose into heaven at His ascension (Acts 1:6–11). Believers are promised we will be like Him! Only God's children—who have the blood of Jesus—can enter this new heaven on the newly created Earth.

> But as for the cowardly, the faithless, the detestable, as for murderers, the sexually immoral, sorcerers, idolaters, and all liars, their portion will be in the lake that burns with fire and sulfur, which is the second death. (Revelation 21:8)

All people from the beginning of creation who do not have the blood of Jesus—who have belonged to Satan from the beginning of time—will be trapped for eternity in the burning physical world. But all those who have washed their robes in the blood of Jesus, whose names are written in the book of life will be welcomed into God's eternal kingdom on Earth.

> Blessed are those who wash their robes, so that they may have the right to the tree of life and that they may enter the city by the gates. Outside are the dogs and sorcerers and the sexually immoral and murderers and idolaters, and everyone who loves and practices falsehood. (Revelation 22:14–15)

*Chapter 2*

# We Are All Pilgrims with a Purpose

THE MOST EXCITING outcome of my Bible research over the past twenty years has been discovering the real reasons God created mankind and the physical world. It has been fascinating to learn that we all pre-existed in heaven and are now pilgrims passing through this world with a very specific and important role as God's people.

My church teaches God created mankind to worship Him and enjoy Him forever. You won't find that in the Bible. The Bible does emphasize the importance of worship, and our worship is a natural reaction once we understand all God has done for us. But if receiving worship from mankind was God's goal for creation, He has been sorely disappointed.

God's ultimate purpose is made clear in Ephesians 1:9–10. He intends to unify the spiritual and physical worlds in Christ:

> [God was] making known to us the mystery of his will, according to his purpose, which he set forth in Christ as a plan for the fullness of time, to unite all things in him, things in heaven and things on earth.

We see the fulfillment of God's purpose in Revelation 21:1:

> Then I saw a new heaven and a new earth, for the first heaven and the first earth had passed away.

God's purpose is to unite the spiritual and the physical worlds into a new heaven on a new Earth, a new world remade to be physical, spiritual, and eternal.

But God's purpose to unite the spiritual and the physical worlds raises the question: "Why did God create the physical world in the first place?" If heaven is perfect, why would God create a physical world filled with sin, suffering, and death? God didn't need millions of lost sinners to worship Him. And He didn't create millions of hopeless sinners to show His love by saving them. There's got to be a better reason—and there is.

Begin by imagining what it was like in the spiritual world before the physical world was created. The Bible tells us "God is light" (1 John 1:5), and the spiritual world is filled with light. And in heaven there is no passage of time, no beginning or end, and no chronological progression of events as we understand it.

> Do not overlook this one fact, beloved, that with the Lord one day is as a thousand years, and a thousand years as one day. (2 Peter 3:8)

God created a large and diverse family of eternal spiritual beings from the highest-ranking seraphim and cherubim as well as the dominions, principalities, archangels, and angels. Based on the description in Revelation of living beings around God's throne, God's spiritual family included billions of beings living in harmony and joy.

These beings freely loved each other and worshipped God. There was no compulsion. All these spiritual beings have become or will become physical bodies and join the long progression of spiritual beings who pass through the physical world on their way to two very different destinations: a new heaven on a new Earth or a physical fiery abyss. What's the reason for this long and difficult journey? God's character requires it.

I'll pause here to give a description of God's character because it reveals His motives and actions throughout the Bible at least to the degree we humans can understand the motives of an infinite God.

Throughout the Bible as a whole, it is evident that God is imbued with four immutable characteristics: love, freedom, justice, and mercy. We see God's unconditional love for His people on display throughout the Bible. God gives His people a free will to choose good or evil. God also gives His people perfect freedom but He is bound by His character to exact perfect justice for our actions—and the just punishment for sin is death (*the wages of sin is death*, according to Romans 6:23). The best news is, God gives His people perfect mercy: He paid the price for our sin with His own life.

From a human perspective, God's character seems full of tension and contradictions. If He really loves us, why would He give us the freedom to choose evil—or even allow evil to exist? It's because His love requires Him to give us freedom to make our own decisions. Why does His justice require such harsh punishment for those He loves? God disciplines those He loves, but He punished Himself for our sin instead of punishing us. That's perfect mercy!

Everything I discuss in this book is impacted by God's character. It seems wrong to limit God in any way but He limits Himself by His own character. God is never arbitrary. Just as He created a universe bound by physical laws, He binds Himself by His immutable character.

Now, back to the very beginning before the creation of the physical world. If the spiritual heaven was perfect, why did God decide to create a physical world? And why do we all have to pass through it? Traditional interpretations of the Bible have made an erroneous assumption resulting in a complete misunderstanding of God's motives. Heaven was not perfect. In fact, sin originated in heaven, and God needed a way to separate evil from His perfect heaven. The physical world created a place to banish Satan from heaven. But separating evil from good was just a part of God's motive for creating the physical world.

God also wanted His spiritual family to have an enhanced eternal physical existence. The physical senses of sight, touch, smell, hearing, and taste, combined with supernatural spiritual characteristics, will provide an eternal existence far beyond anything we can imagine.

Jesus serves as our prototype of what God intends for all His family. Jesus began as a spiritual being, as the very voice of God.

> In the beginning was the Word, and the Word was with God, and the Word was God. He was in the beginning with God. All things

> were made through him, and without him was not anything made that was made. In him was life, and the life was the light of men. (John 1:1–4)

The spiritual Jesus—God's voice—became a physical man:

> The Word became flesh and dwelt among us, and we have seen his glory, glory as of the only Son from the Father, full of grace and truth. (John 1:14)

The resurrected Jesus was both spiritual and physical. He could pass through walls and disappear, but He was also completely physical:

> Although the doors were locked, Jesus came and stood among them and said, "Peace be with you." Then he said to Thomas, "Put your finger here, and see my hands; and put out your hand, and place it in my side. Do not disbelieve, but believe." (John 20:26–27)

The resurrected Jesus could eat fish (physical) as well as vanish, reappear in a distant place and, later, ascend to heaven (spiritual; see Luke 24:31 and Acts 1:9–12). Jesus gave us a glimpse of what God wants for His whole family. Like Jesus, all of us began in heaven (although we are created beings and Jesus is the eternal God). God knew us long before the physical world was created:

> Blessed be the God and Father of our Lord Jesus Christ, who has blessed us in Christ with every spiritual blessing in the heavenly places, even as he chose us in him before the foundation of the world, that we should be holy and blameless before him. In love he predestined us for adoption to himself as sons through Jesus Christ, according to the purpose of his will, to the praise of his glorious grace, with which he has blessed us in the Beloved. (Ephesians 1:3–6)

When spiritual beings become human, the Bible refers to them as *sons*. Even Satan's fallen angels were called *sons of God* when they became human (Genesis 6:2). Jesus is the only Son of God because He *is* God. God chose a select group of spiritual beings (I believe these were the angels who fought against Satan in the war in heaven) to become His adopted sons in Jesus. This suggests that two-thirds of modern humans are God's chosen people. When God's chosen people on Earth repent and accept Jesus as their savior, God adopts them as His own sons (men and women), and we are restored to His family. Jesus calls us His brothers (this, of course, includes women)!

Humans are a physical projection or image of spiritual beings. In fact, everything in the physical world is an image of something in the spiritual world. The verse below from Hebrews implies that the universe was created out of things that already existed but were invisible:

> By faith we understand that the universe was created by the word of God, so that what is seen was not made out of things that are visible. (Hebrews 11:3)

The spiritual and physical worlds exist simultaneously as demonstrated when the physical Jesus lived on Earth concurrently with God the Father and Holy Spirit in heaven. Every human is an image of a spiritual counterpart, so God's people on Earth have a co-existing spiritual counterpart in heaven. Satan's people on Earth carry their evil spiritual counterparts within them (because they were thrown out of heaven), and when their bodies die, their spirits are trapped in the physical world in what the Bible calls the abyss. There is no resurrection for Satan's people except when they face Judgment Day.

God's people first lived as spirits in heaven. Then, as He did in Jesus, God made physical images of our spiritual beings. But because the physical world is separated from God by sin, our physical beings are separated from God and from our own spiritual selves. The only way we can be reunited with God and with our own spirits is by repenting of our sinful nature and asking Jesus to cleanse us with His blood, the only physical and spiritual blood. Jesus's blood purifies our physical bodies, gives us His Holy Spirit to live within us, and reconnects us to God the Father in heaven. This is part of God's plan to unify heaven and Earth. So when our physical bodies die, we will be resurrected like Jesus with perfect physical and spiritual bodies.

We pass through the physical world as exiles from heaven and pilgrims on Earth on our way to the Promised Land, to the new heaven on a new Earth. Our lives didn't begin on Earth, and our lives don't end when our bodies die. Our faith is founded on the understanding that we are pilgrims in a dark and sinful land seeking our future home in the kingdom of God. As is written in the book of Hebrews, we will not receive God's promises in this life but He has prepared a city where all His promises will be fulfilled:

> These all died in faith, not having received the things promised, but having seen them and greeted them from afar, and having acknowledged that they were strangers and exiles on

> the earth. For people who speak thus make it clear that they are seeking a homeland. If they had been thinking of that land from which they had gone out, they would have had opportunity to return. But as it is, they desire a better country, that is, a heavenly one. Therefore God is not ashamed to be called their God, for he has prepared for them a city. (Hebrews 11:13–16)

Paul said spiritual beings living temporarily in physical bodies is like living in a tent:

> For we know that if the tent that is our earthly home is destroyed, we have a building from God, a house not made with hands, eternal in the heavens. For in this tent we groan, longing to put on our heavenly dwelling, if indeed by putting it on we may not be found naked. For while we are still in this tent, we groan, being burdened—not that we would be unclothed, but that we would be further clothed, so that what is mortal may be swallowed up by life. He who has prepared us for this very thing is God, who has given us the Spirit as a guarantee.
>
> So we are always of good courage. We know that while we are at home in the body

> we are away from the Lord, for we walk by faith, not by sight. Yes, we are of good courage, and we would rather be away from the body and at home with the Lord. So whether we are at home or away, we make it our aim to please him. For we must all appear before the judgment seat of Christ, so that each one may receive what is due for what he has done in the body, whether good or evil. (2 Corinthians 5:1–10)

God illustrated our pilgrimage in temporary physical bodies by living in a tent among His people when the Jews were in the desert. The Tent of Meeting provided a temporary dwelling for the Ark of the Covenant, God's home on Earth. And just as God lived in a more permanent physical temple once the Jews settled in the Promised Land, God will one day become an eternal temple for His people.

Why must we pass through this dark land of sin and death? Because we must have physical and spiritual characteristics before we can live in the physical and spiritual heaven. When Jesus said we must be *born of water and the Spirit* before we can enter His kingdom, He was saying we had to be born as both spiritual and physical beings (water is symbolic of the physical world):

> Jesus answered, "Truly, truly, I say to you, unless one is born of water and the Spirit, he cannot enter the kingdom of God." (John 3:5)

God used His physical people, the Jews, to show us the journey we must take as His spiritual people. The Jews began in the Promised Land (as we began in heaven), but because of famine, they were forced to go to Egypt (as we are sent to Earth perhaps because of the war in heaven) to be saved. But the Jews became slaves in Egypt just as God's people become slaves to sin on Earth. Egypt both saved the Jews and forced them into slavery just as Earth saved God's people by allowing them to be *born of water* but also forced them into slavery to sin.

God used Moses to save the Jews from slavery in Egypt just as God used Jesus to save His people from slavery to sin on Earth. But the Jews did not have the faith to enter the Promised Land, and a whole generation of Jews died in the desert just as many of God's people on Earth never have the faith to trust Jesus for salvation and fail to be reconnected with God while they live on Earth. (We will discuss more about salvation in later chapters.)

Another reason God's people must pass through the tribulations of this life on Earth is because we must continue to participate in the war between good and evil in order to defeat Satan. The great war in heaven described in Revelation continues on Earth, and the outcome will depend on the faithfulness of God's people. **The angels who were loyal to God, fought against Satan, and cast Satan out of heaven are God's chosen people on Earth. We are the physical images of the angels who chose to be loyal to God!** I believe all God's people on Earth have a spiritual counterpart in heaven who is an angel:

> See that you do not despise one of these little ones. For I tell you that in heaven their angels always see the face of my Father who is in heaven. (Matthew18:10)

God must allow His people to be a part of the war between good and evil because Satan demands that He allow freedom and justice. Satan accused God of not giving His people the freedom to choose good or evil, to choose whether to follow God or Satan. And Satan also continuously accuses God's people of worshipping God simply because He bribes them with His blessings.

In Revelation we learn Satan is always accusing the *brothers*:

> Now the salvation and the power and the kingdom of our God and the authority of his Christ have come, for the accuser of our

> brothers has been thrown down, who accuses them day and night before our God. (Revelation 12:10)

In Job—which is an allegory for all mankind—we learn the details of Satan's accusations. Satan accused God of bribing His people to get their worship and of not giving us the freedom to choose good or evil. He also accused God's people of worshipping and obeying God only because God blesses them:

> Then Satan answered the Lord and said, "Does Job fear God for no reason? Have you not put a hedge around him and his house and all that he has, on every side? You have blessed the work of his hands, and his possessions have increased in the land. But stretch out your hand and touch all that he has, and he will curse you to your face." (Job 1:9–11)

Satan appealed to God's character of freedom and justice. That's another reason all God's people must travel through this sinful physical life filled with suffering and death. We are here to answer Satan's accusations, to prove Satan wrong, to defeat Satan and his demons, and to justify God's salvation. We are here to prove God right!

God doesn't need to be justified or proven right, but His character requires Him to allow the war between evil and good to play out on Earth. And the outcome of this great war depends on God's people. God is not fighting this war; His people are. How do God's people participate in the war between evil and good? We obey God, not Satan. The book of Job provides many lessons for believers.

If you accept Job as an allegory for your own life, then you began in heaven. In the beginning of the book of Job, he was clearly living in a type of heaven on Earth. But Satan's challenge to God results in Job—like all of us—going through the great tribulations of physical life. Just like Job, every human goes through tragedy, suffering, and death. Yet, despite his suffering and complaints, Job stayed faithful to God and proved Satan wrong. Satan is defeated, and God is proved right. And in the end Job is restored to a new heaven on Earth that is even more wonderful than where he began. Job began in heaven, suffered through terrible tribulation, and ended up in a new and better heaven. That is the journey for all God's people.

When God's people obey His commands, pray, and worship, we participate in the process of defeating Satan. When we praise God, especially in the middle of suffering and pain, we weaken Satan's hold on God's people. When we love each other and love God despite all the troubles we face in the world, we help win the war between good and evil.

All God's people must understand the seriousness of our roles in this great war. It is a mistake not to fight in this war because we think it's all in God's hands. God put it all in the hands of His people. God has given Jesus all authority on heaven and Earth but Jesus has delegated His power to His body, the Church. We are His hands, feet, and voices on Earth. The outcome of the war between evil and good depends on us!

*Chapter 3*

# The Real Creation Story

CHRISTIANS ARE PRESENTED with an uncomfortable intellectual choice between either God-directed creation or accidental origins and random evolution. Some Christians try to resolve the tension between these two opposing "truths" by fabricating a hybrid of God-directed evolution that comports with neither science nor the Bible. The big problem for Christians: if the biblical version of creation is not true, then the Bible is not true, and our faith is useless.

Can the biblical version of creation be reconciled with credible science? Absolutely! In fact, the existence and continuation of the universe cannot be explained without recognizing everything is being held together by an unseen spiritual energy.

Scientific analysis of the physical universe focuses on matter and phenomena that can be seen, observed, and studied. Science also studies unseen phenomena, such as gravity and energy, that can be analyzed indirectly based on their observable effects on physical matter. But science has developed very little understanding of the large majority of the physical universe because it can't be seen or explained. According to scientists, 95 percent of the universe doesn't exist! (Keep reading!)

I won't fill this book with excerpts from scientific journals but it's important to point out the large blind spot most scientists have when it comes to understanding the physical universe and how it originated. When scientists begin their study of creation with the assumption there is no God and no spiritual or metaphysical dimension, they rule out the only rational hypothesis to explain the existence of the physical universe.

All matter is composed of mostly empty space. Even a piece of steel is composed of tiny atoms with lots of empty space between them and empty space within them. These atoms are always in motion, and no one can explain where the energy comes from that keeps an uncountable number of atoms in perpetual motion throughout the universe.

The empty spaces throughout the universe are called dark matter and dark energy by scientists. Wikipedia (not always the most reliable resource) has a well-sourced analysis of dark matter that explains how 95 percent of the universe doesn't exist at least in a physical sense. Here's one excerpt:

> In the standard lambda-CDM model of cosmology, the mass-energy content of the universe is 5% ordinary matter, 26.8% dark matter, and 68.2% a form of energy known as dark energy. Thus, dark matter constitutes 85% of the total mass, while dark energy and dark matter constitute 95% of the total mass–energy content.

Scientists indirectly acknowledge the universe is filled with spiritual matter and energy that holds everything together. The Bible tells us the same thing: Jesus holds all things together. He created all things, and *in him all things hold together*:

> He is the image of the invisible God, the firstborn of all creation. For by him all things were created, in heaven and on earth, visible and invisible, whether thrones or dominions or rulers or authorities—all things were created through him and for him. And he is before all things, and in him all things hold together. And he is the head of the body, the church. He is the beginning, the firstborn from the dead, that in everything he might be preeminent. For in him all the fullness of God was pleased to dwell, and through him to reconcile to himself all things, whether on earth or

> in heaven, making peace by the blood of his cross. (Colossians 1:15–20)

The Bible tells us Jesus fills all the empty space in the universe. The dark matter and energy in the universe are the Spirit of Jesus:

> He [God the Father] put all things under his [Jesus's] feet and gave him as head over all things to the church, which is his body, the fullness of him who fills all in all. (Ephesians 1:22–23)

Also, Jesus fills with His Holy Spirit everyone who invites Him into their hearts as Savior and Lord. Jesus fills all their emptiness!

> In him we live and move and have our being. (Acts 17:28)

With all this in mind, as we assess the Genesis account of creation, it is important to know the physical universe exists within the spiritual world. Everything visible in the physical world is a projection—or an image—of something invisible in the spiritual world. The spiritual and physical worlds are intertwined and continuously connected.

The physical universe must be understood not only as an image of the spiritual world but as a bridge or passage to a new heaven on a new Earth. Everything in the spiritual world will pass through the physical world before the current spiritual and physical worlds end. In addition, the physical world is the battlefield for the war between good and evil being fought between God's people and Satan's people.

## Major Concepts in Genesis 1

There are several major concepts in the first chapter of Genesis that provide insights into how God created the physical universe:

| *Concept* | *Meaning* |
|---|---|
| *In the beginning* before spiritual matter became physical images | Verses 1 and 2 describe physical matter being spread throughout an infinite universe. There was no formed *Earth*, only atoms mixed within a *void* of spiritual dark matter and dark energy—described as *the Spirit of God hovering over the face of the waters* (Genesis 1:2). Importantly, the future Earth was initially a massive cloud of water mixed with matter that would later clump into a solid sphere. All this likely developed over a long period of time before the first so-called day. |

| Concept | Meaning |
| --- | --- |
| *Days* | This term most likely refers to periods of time, not twenty-four-hour days. Genesis 2:4 summarizes the seven days as generations. There was, for instance, no sun until the Day 4, so these are unlikely twenty-four-hour days. The phrase *evening and morning* refers to the end of one period of time and the beginning of another. (Evening to morning is twelve hours of night, so the phrase doesn't appear to be describing a twenty-four-hour day.) |
| *God said* | God's voice or word is described as Jesus many places in the Bible. Jesus—God's physical presence on Earth—spoke everything into existence. |
| *Let there be light* | Jesus described Himself as *the light of the world* and *the light of life.*[1] When God said, *"Let there be light,"* He was filling the universe with the spirit of Jesus. This was not the light from the sun. It was God opening the portals of heaven and allowing His light to fill the universe. The light sustained all life on Earth until the sun was created. |

*Separated*

The physical world provided a way to separate things. Apparently, separation is not part of the spiritual world where there is no separation between life and death (there is no death) or between good and evil. In Genesis 1, God separated heaven and earth; light and darkness; day and night; evening and morning; water over and water under the sky; dry land and seas; plants and trees according to their kinds; seasons; different kinds of living creatures; male and female; and physical images from spiritual beings.

*Good* and *very good*

God declared each progression of His work *good*, and when creation was complete, He declared it all *very good*. This was God's certification there was nothing bad—there was no evil—in the physical universe. This is a definitive statement that Satan and his demons had not yet been thrown down, and there was no evil in the world.

*God's rest*

God wasn't tired after He created the physical world. His *rest* was an illustration of the promised rest prepared for all His people[2]. From creation until the end of time, God has called and is calling His people to enter His promised rest—to come to Him for salvation from this sinful world. The seventh day of rest in Genesis lasted many years and provided peace and happiness for all creation, representing our future heaven on Earth.

I should clarify several points related to creation. First, the biblical version of creation will not align with all the chronological events theorized by some evolutionary scientists because they have a huge blind spot: in their hypothesis, they do not allow for the existence of God or the metaphysical (spiritual). Their conclusions defy the laws of physics, biology, statistical probability, and common sense. Evolutionary science has been discredited and modified multiple times since Darwin introduced the theory in 1859.

Second, because the physical universe is essentially a projection or image of things in the spiritual world, the entire creation process may have happened in an instant. So the *days* in Genesis could easily be twenty-four-hour periods. God didn't need generations to complete the creation process, but an instant to God may well have been thousands of years in the physical world.

Third, because the physical world was created or imaged from pre-existing spiritual matter, carbon dating or other methods used to determine age in the physical world may be heavily skewed. It is also likely that the winding down of atomic matter does not occur at a consistent rate over thousands of years, making it an unreliable measurement of age. Carbon dating has been found to be inaccurate in many studies.[3]

Fourth, the creation of humans reported in Genesis 1 is not the same account as the creation of Adam and Eve in Genesis 2. (I will explain this conclusion in the next chapter.) The biblical determination of the age of the earth should therefore not be measured from the time of Adam and Eve because they were created thousands or even millions of years after the creation of early humans.

## Creation According to Genesis

### *Before the First So-Called Day*

> In the beginning, God created the heavens and the earth. The earth was without form and void, and darkness was over the face of the deep. And the Spirit of God was hovering over the face of the waters. (Genesis 1:1–2)

The spiritual world is like a digital file on a computer. When God began to create the physical world, He was booting parts of a spiritual file onto a display screen, and the invisible became visible.

When the spiritual world was booted up as the physical world, spiritual eternity became physical infinity. Our infinite universe is evidence of the existence of eternity. Science concludes time and space are *inextricably linked*:

> Einstein . . . introduced the concept of time as the fourth dimension, which meant that space and time were inextricably linked. His general theory of relativity suggests that space-time expands and contracts depending on the momentum and mass of nearby matter.[4]

The concept of limitless time (eternity) fits with the concept of limitless space (an infinite physical universe). This reality supports God's promise that when the spiritual and physical worlds are united as the new heaven, God's people will enjoy eternal life in physical bodies in an infinite physical space.

The first step of creation was the transfer of dark matter and dark energy into the physical dimension, along with physical matter, including water. The universe was mostly void (empty), dark, and cold. There was no formed Earth because physical matter had not yet clumped into planets and suns.

Science theorizes that physical matter, like atomic dust, swirled into millions of separate massive disks throughout the universe. Over time, the physical matter collided and clumped together to form suns followed by planets.[5] This chronology certainly fits with the biblical account. Science, however, concludes that stars (suns) were formed before planets. Genesis describes the creation of Earth before the sun, but the sun may have been created as a sphere long before God made it a light on the fourth "day."

God created the universe with fixed laws of physics, so it is likely He allowed the formation of suns and planets to develop naturally according to physical laws over millions of years which in the spiritual world may have seemed like a day. This initial phase of creation occurred before the first "day" that began when God said, "Let there be light."

### *"Day" 1*

On the first "day," God's light was unleashed as an explosion of energy into the physical world. This was not the light of the sun (the sun became a light on the fourth "day"). God's light in the universe was the life-giving light of God—that also created heat to warm the universe—described in Revelation 22:5:

> And night will be no more. They will need no light of lamp or sun, for the Lord God will be their light, and they will reign forever and ever.

This verse from Revelation also helps explain other aspects of "Day" 1. The earth was not yet a solid sphere. God didn't create regular days and nights governed by the sun until "Day" 4. On "Day" 1, God replaced the darkness in the universe with light. He called the light

*Day*, but this light was continuous with no nighttime period of darkness because the whole universe was filled with His light. The past darkness was separated from the light and called the *Night.* (According to Revelation 22:5, the long period of night was *no more.*)

> God saw that the light was good. And God separated the light from the darkness. God called the light Day, and the darkness he called Night. (Genesis 1:4–5)

### *"Day" 2*

The earth became a fiery sphere surrounded by a cloud of superheated water vapor extending hundreds of miles above the surface. As the earth cooled, water vapor condensed and fell to the surface. This created a large expanse of clear sky above the earth. A thick layer of water vapor remained hundreds of miles above the surface:

> God said, "Let there be an expanse in the midst of the waters, and let it separate the waters from the waters." And God made the expanse and separated the waters that were under the expanse from the waters that were above the expanse. (Genesis 1:6–7)

Earth was unique among all the planets because of the large quantities of water around it. Our world is still known as "the water planet."

The residual large quantity of water vapor high above the earth created greenhouse tropical conditions all around the globe. And importantly, the massive amounts of water above the atmosphere explain the source of the water that eventually fell and covered the entire earth during the Great Flood of Noah's time. This canopy of water vapor may have provided protection from ultraviolet rays from the sun, partially explaining long lifespans before the flood.

### *"Day" 3*

The waters that fell to the earth during the second *day* gathered into small seas around the globe on "Day" 3. Much of this falling water also drained into large underground caverns that still exist as underground seas today. These caverns were formed as the earth cooled and created a Swiss-cheese subterranean infrastructure.

> God said, "Let the waters under the heavens be gathered together into one place, and let the dry land appear." And it was so. God called the dry land Earth, and the waters that were gathered together he called Seas." (Genesis 1:9–10)

We know much of the water on Earth at this time drained below the surface because Genesis 2:6 tells us that there was no rain and the whole Earth was watered by a mist coming up from the ground.

The tropical climate and moist soil created ideal conditions for plants and trees to flourish:

> God said, "Let the earth sprout vegetation, plants yielding seed, and fruit trees bearing fruit in which is their seed, each according to its kind, on the earth." And it was so. The earth brought forth vegetation, plants yielding seed according to their own kinds, and trees bearing fruit in which is their seed, each according to its kind. And God saw that it was good." (Genesis 1:11–12)

Evolutionary scientists theorize a single cell somehow formed and came to life millions of years ago, likely in a pool of primordial slime. This living cell somehow survived without food, reproduced itself, and, over millions of years, figured out how to come together with other cells to form more complex organisms. There is absolutely no "scientific" evidence that this occurred. In fact, the formation of a living cell from inorganic material is impossible. The accidental formation of a living cell with the ability to reproduce is impossible, and the spontaneous organization of autonomous cells into complex organisms is preposterous. It is criminal these theories are taught in our schools under the guise of "science."

### *"Day" 4*

It is important to note plants were growing all around the earth before the creation of the sun. God filled the universe with His life-giving light, and no sun was necessary just as, according to the description in Revelation of the new heaven, no sun will be needed because God's light will fill the universe.

I believe the physical sphere we call the sun existed before Earth became a sphere on "Day" 2. On "Day" 4, God lit the sun on fire, initiating the nuclear fusion that generates heat and light.

> God said, "Let there be lights in the expanse of the heavens to separate the day from the night. And let them be for signs and for seasons, and for days and years, and let them be lights in the expanse of the heavens to give light upon the earth." And it was so. And God made the two great lights—the greater light to rule the day and the lesser light to rule the night—and the stars. And God set them in the expanse of the heavens to give light on the earth, to rule over the day and over the night, and to

> separate the light from the darkness. And God saw that it was good. (Genesis 1:14–18)

Earth's atmosphere likely contained high concentrations of $CO_2$ that joined with warm, humid air and moist soil to create the perfect conditions for plants to thrive.

A long time ago, before humans, dinosaurs, plants, or even bacteria, Earth's air had no oxygen. If we could time travel to that period, we would need space suits to breathe. Scientists think the air was mostly made out of volcanic gases like carbon dioxide.[6]

If God allowed the development process to proceed naturally, it would have taken millions of years for photosynthesis by plant life to fill Earth's atmosphere and seas with oxygen. Only then was Earth ready to sustain animal life.

### *"Day" 5*

Most scientists will agree that animal life began in the water and that birds likely preceded other animal life on Earth, although new theories suggest prehistoric birds evolved from a type of running dinosaur. The fact is, scientists don't know. The biblical progression of creation makes more common sense:

> God said, "Let the waters swarm with swarms of living creatures, and let birds fly above the

> earth across the expanse of the heavens." So God created the great sea creatures and every living creature that moves, with which the waters swarm, according to their kinds, and every winged bird according to its kind. And God saw that it was good. (Genesis 1:20–21)

### *"Day" 6*

The sixth period of creation began with God creating animals and reptiles on Earth:

> God said, "Let the earth bring forth living creatures according to their kinds—livestock and creeping things and beasts of the earth according to their kinds." (Genesis 1:24)

The next phase of creation—the creation of humans—is perhaps the most misunderstood part of the Bible. When God said, *"Let us make man,"* He was obviously speaking to an audience of heavenly hosts:

> Then God said, "Let us make man in our image, after our likeness." (Genesis 1:26)

God appears to be saying to the angelic hosts, "Let us make physical images of ourselves." Some theologians conclude God used the plural *us* because He was speaking to Himself as the Trinity. However, God is *one* (Deuteronomy 6:4), and it is unlikely He would refer to Himself as separate spiritual beings. When Jesus was a man, He did refer to His spiritual Father as a separate being in heaven, but He said He and the Father *are one* (John10:30).

The angelic hosts around God included a hierarchy of beings the Bible generically calls angels. As God's creations, these beings all share the image of God. That's why God said, "*Let us create man in our image*" (Genesis 1:26). And that's why creating man in God's image includes the image of God's family.

> So God created man in his own image,
> in the image of God he created him;
> male and female he created them. (Genesis 1:27)

The highest-ranking angels are seraphim and cherubim (Satan is a cherubim). Other angels were called *thrones, dominions, virtues, powers, principalities, archangels*, and *angels*. I'm confident there are many other levels of spiritual beings in heaven the Bible doesn't mention. Based on the images of animals presented in heaven in the book of Revelation, it is possible animals on Earth may be the physical images of heavenly beings. (Apparently every physical being is important to God: a sparrow doesn't fall to the ground without God's notice [Matthew 10:29]!).

All spiritual beings will eventually become physical beings that live and die on Earth. When God created the first humans, they were likely images of the lower hierarchy of angels. And, I suspect, they were much more advanced and physically attractive than the prehistoric humans presented by scientists.

The imaging of angels to humans has occurred over many generations because spiritual beings had to wait for humans to *be fruitful and multiply* (Genesis 1:28). There was a progression of spiritual beings moving through the physical world as the first humans thousands of years before Adam and Eve.

### *"Day" 7*

God finished His initial creation hundreds of thousands of years ago. The earth was perfect. Humans and animals lived in perfect harmony. There was no sin in the world, and all physical beings were consciously united with the spiritual world, their spiritual counterparts, and God. There was no spiritual death, but I'm guessing their physical bodies were mortal and died. This was necessary for a large quantity of spirits to pass through the physical world. There was no fear of death because spiritual life was continuous, and physical death was little more than changing clothes. When all was finished, God rested from His work. God invites all His children to enter His rest:

> Thus the heavens and the earth were finished, and all the host of them. And on the seventh day God finished his work that he had done, and he rested on the seventh day from all his work that he had done. So God blessed the seventh day and made it holy, because on it God rested from all his work that he had done in creation. (Genesis 2:1–3)

## *Chapter 4*

# Satan's Rebellion, Devastation on Earth, and Adam and Eve

WHEN GOD FINISHED His creation and rested, the Bible summarizes the creation account this way:

> These are the generations
> of the heavens and the earth when they were created,
> in the day that the Lord God made the earth and the heavens.
> (Genesis 2:4)

Traditional interpretation of this verse assumes it is a preamble to all that follows, to the generations of Adam and Eve and their offspring. However, this interpretation defies the actual text. The verse actually closes the Genesis description of the *generations of the heavens and the earth when they were created.* What follows this verse has nothing to do with the creation of heaven and Earth. Genesis 2:4 is obviously a wrap-up statement about the generational periods ("days") of creation in the first chapter of Genesis. We should also note this verse refers to all the generations of creation as *the day*. Days are being used to describe long periods of time.

The Bible is the inspired Word of God, but the chapter and verse designations are not inspired and can be misleading. In this case, Genesis 1 should have continued to Genesis 2:4 to include the Genesis 2:4 closing statement about creation. Chapter 2 should begin with Genesis 2:5, the beginning of a new story.

The whole world changed dramatically between Genesis 2:4 and 2:5!

The book of Revelation (a detailed review of Revelation is included in a later chapter) helps us see that thousands—perhaps millions—of years passed between verses 2:4 and 2:5. This period of time after creation is when Satan was thrown down to Earth. Excerpts from Revelation reveal why and when Satan rebelled against God and how he was banished from heaven. Satan was jealous of God's Son—Jesus—who was destined to rule heaven and Earth. So Satan pursued the woman who would give birth to Jesus:

> A great sign appeared in heaven: a woman clothed with the sun, with the moon under her feet, and on her head a crown of twelve stars. She was pregnant and was crying out in birth pains and the agony of giving birth. (Revelation 12:1–2)

The woman in this verse is the spiritual mother of the physical line of Jesus. She is God's creative force on Earth, surrounded by the physical creations described in Genesis 1: the sun, the moon, and the stars. The woman is a biblical type pointing to Eve, the mother of modern humans, and to Mary, the mother of Jesus. This woman in Revelation gives birth to God's voice: His Son and the first physical manifestation of Jesus on Earth.

Also known as Lucifer and one of God's most trusted and powerful angels, Satan was jealous of God's Son and wanted to kill Him. Satan may have believed by killing the physical Jesus, he would also kill God the Father and be free to replace Him as ruler over heaven and Earth. The dragon in Revelation is Satan:

> The dragon stood before the woman who was about to give birth, so that when she bore her child he might devour it. She gave birth to a male child, one who is to rule all the nations with a rod of iron, but her child was caught up

> to God and to his throne, and the woman fled into the wilderness, where she has a place prepared by God, in which she is to be nourished for 1,260 days. (Revelation 12:4–6)

This account from Revelation is the first advent of the physical Jesus. Jesus referred to Himself as *the first and the last* (Revelation 1:17), so it seems likely Jesus was born into the physical world before the creation of Adam as this passage suggests and was taken to heaven for protection. Jesus was the invincible God in the spiritual world, but the physical Jesus could be killed by Satan (as we saw much later in the crucifixion). Jesus was later born to Mary and will ultimately return as the last spiritual being to pass through the physical world. Jesus *was, is and is to come,* indicating that He lives continuously in the past, present, and future (Revelation 1:8). He is *the Alpha and the Omega, the first and the last* (Revelation 22:13).

Satan's rebellion against God and his attempt to kill Jesus led to a war in heaven. One-third of all the angels in heaven fought on Satan's side against the angels loyal to God:[1]

> Now war arose in heaven, Michael and his angels fighting against the dragon. And the dragon and his angels fought back, but he was defeated, and there was no longer any place

> for them in heaven. And the great dragon was thrown down, that ancient serpent, who is called the devil and Satan, the deceiver of the whole world—he was thrown down to the earth, and his angels were thrown down with him. (Revelation 12:7–9)

After Jesus was taken to heaven for protection, Satan continued to pursue the woman and her offspring on Earth. But God provided a place of protection, namely—the Garden of Eden.

We can deduce when Satan was thrown out of heaven and down to Earth. It had to be after the seven "Days" of creation because God pronounced all the physical world *very good*. There was no sin in the world when God rested on the seventh "Day." Satan was thrown down to Earth after creation but before the Garden of Eden and before Adam and Eve. In fact, the evil and destruction that resulted from Satan's arrival on Earth was the reason the Garden of Eden was necessary.

When Satan and his angels were thrown out of heaven, Earth was devastated by the collision of spiritual evil into the physical world. Heaven was purified, but the inhabitants of Earth were warned of Satan's great wrath:

> I [the apostle John] heard a loud voice in heaven, saying, "Now the salvation and the

> power and the kingdom of our God and the authority of his Christ have come, for the accuser of our brothers has been thrown down, who accuses them day and night before our God. And they have conquered him by the blood of the Lamb and by the word of their testimony, for they loved not their lives even unto death. Therefore, rejoice, O heavens and you who dwell in them! But woe to you, O earth and sea, for the devil has come down to you in great wrath, because he knows that his time is short!" (Revelation 12:10–12)

The first five trumpets in Revelation 8 and 9 describe the devastation on Earth when Satan and his angels are thrown down.

> Hail and fire, mixed with blood . . . were thrown upon the earth. And a third of the earth was burned up, and a third of the trees were burned up, and all green grass was burned up.
>
> A great mountain, burning with fire, was thrown into the sea, and a third of the sea became blood. A third of the living creatures in the sea died, and a third of the ships were destroyed.

> A great star fell from heaven, blazing like a torch, and it fell on a third of the rivers and on the springs of water. The name of the star is Wormwood. A third of the waters became wormwood, and many people died from the water, because it had been made bitter.
>
> A third of the sun was struck, and a third of the moon, and a third of the stars, so that a third of their light might be darkened, and a third of the day might be kept from shining, and likewise a third of the night. . . .
>
> I saw a star fallen from heaven to earth, and he [the angel] was given the key to the shaft of the bottomless pit. He opened the shaft of the bottomless pit, and from the shaft rose smoke like the smoke of a great furnace, and the sun and the air were darkened with the smoke from the shaft. Then from the smoke came locusts on the earth, and they were given power like the power of scorpions of the earth (Revelation 8:7–12, 9:1–3).

Scientists seek to explain ice ages that occurred hundreds of thousands of years ago and the disappearance of dinosaurs with theories of asteroids hitting Earth, creating global dust clouds, and blocking the sun for thousands of years. The Bible tells us what really happened.

When Satan and his demons were thrown out of heaven, the tropical paradise on Earth was destroyed. Most humans, animals, and plant life died. Satan brought evil to Earth and separated early humans from God and the spiritual world. Fallen angels—called *sons of God*—took on human form and ruled the world. Humans suffered from lack of sunshine and nutrition. Humans began to eat meat, and animals began to eat each other. Conditions on Earth were horrible for thousands of years. Many humans lived in caves, hiding from animals that sought to eat them. The earth was dark, cold, violent, and evil.

God needed a protected place for His creation of modern humans, the line through which God's people and the eventual mother of Jesus would come. God called this protected place a garden in Eden. God placed Adam, the first modern human, in Eden. Adam was the first physical image of God's highest ranking and most powerful angels who would become modern humans through Adam and his descendants. We know the creation of Adam is different from the creation of early humans because his formation is described in a completely different way (Genesis 2:7) than the creation of early humans (Genesis 1:26–27).

After the creation account is summarized in Genesis 2:4, the next verse begins to describe a different situation on Earth. Some Bible translations (the NIV and NASB, for instance) begin verse 2:5 with the word *Now*, suggesting that what follows is something different from what was previously described:

> Now no shrub of the field was yet in the earth,
> and no plant of the field had yet sprouted,
> for the Lord God had not sent rain upon the earth, and there was no man to cultivate the ground. (Genesis 2:5 NASB)

God created plant life all around the world on the third *day* before early humans were created on the sixth *day,* so the verse above is not saying there were no plants before Adam was created. Instead, the verse is clearly saying there were no cultivated crops grown by early humans. Adam needed to plant seeds, grow crops, and harvest food because Satan had destroyed much of the naturally growing plants on Earth.

Here are some key differences between the description of Adam and early humans:

| *Adam* | *Early Humans* |
| --- | --- |
| Adam was referred to as ***the man*** in Genesis 2:7. | Early humans were referred to generically as *mankind* in Genesis 1:26. |
| Adam was formed from the ground as a separate individual, and God personally breathed life into his body (Genesis 2:7). | Early humans were created en masse as images of spiritual beings, male and female at the same time (Genesis 1:27). |
| Adam was the first human to cultivate crops (Genesis 2:15). | Early humans were scavengers finding food on trees and plants all around them (Genesis 1:29). They didn't eat meat until Satan was thrown down to Earth. |
| The Garden of Eden included the presence of evil—*the tree of the knowledge of good and evil*—and Satan had access to the garden (Genesis 2:9 and 3:1). | There was no evil in the world when early humans were created: it was all *very good* (Genesis 1:31). |
| For a period of time, Adam lived alone in the garden with the modern animals God created (Genesis 2:18). | Male and female early humans were created at the same time (Genesis 1:27). |

| ***Adam*** | ***Early Humans*** |
|---|---|
| The first modern female human (Eve) was formed from a part of *the man*—Adam. Eve was the first *woman*. | Early human females were created in the image of God at the same time as males. |
| Adam and Eve chose to gain the knowledge of evil (Genesis 3:6). | Early humans lived with no evil or sin until Satan arrived on Earth, God had said all of His creation was *very good*. |
| Adam and his family raised sheep for meat (Genesis 4:2–4). | Early humans only ate the plants —fruit, seeds, and vegetables—growing around them (Genesis 1:29). |

Adam and Eve were created in a perfect environment. They were connected to their spiritual counterparts in heaven and enjoyed a personal relationship with God. Jesus, God's physical image, actually walked in the Garden with Adam and Eve.[2]

Satan demanded that God—and God's character required Him to—allow Adam and Eve to suffer and to have the freedom to choose between good and evil, the freedom to choose between God and Satan.[3] This is why there had to be a *tree of the knowledge of good and evil* in the Garden of Eden. God commanded Adam not to eat from this one tree and told him he would die if he did. We don't know how well Adam explained this to Eve!

Apparently Satan took the form of a serpent and spoke to Eve. This suggests Adam and Eve may have been able to communicate with the animals in the garden because there is no indication it was unusual for the snake to talk to Eve.

Satan twisted the truth just enough to confuse Eve. Adam was standing next to her and didn't help the situation. Eve probably didn't know that eating from the tree would cause her to die spiritually—to be separated from God and heaven. She also had no idea of the pain and suffering her act would bring to the whole human race as she invited evil into her life.

> The serpent said to the woman, "You will not surely die. For God knows that when you eat of it your eyes will be opened, and you will be like God, knowing good and evil." (Genesis 3:4–5)

When Adam and Eve ate the fruit from the tree of the knowledge of good and evil, they died spiritually and immediately became conscious of their nakedness, of their sin and separation from God. They were ashamed to be seen by God.[4]

After Adam and Eve's disobedience, the presence of evil on Earth revealed itself in many ways. Adam and Eve were banished from the Garden of Eden. Food was hard to grow and find: it now required a lot of work and frustration. Childbirth would involve a lot of pain, and their physical bodies would die and return to dust. But the worst part of Eve's act was the surrender of the physical world to Satan. The world was now the dominion of Satan, and every human would be born with a sin nature, separated from God and the spiritual world.

All humans—except Jesus—would have a sin nature until the end of time, and many would be born as children of Satan, as the images of fallen angels. We know this because the first modern human born in this world—Cain—was *of the evil one* (1 John 3:12). Cain was a son of Satan! Cain killed his brother Abel because God approved of Abel's sacrifice but did not accept Cain's.[5]

God banished Cain to live with the surviving early humans and Satan's fallen angels—those *sons of God*. This began the battle between good and evil on Earth and the countdown to the promised Savior.

## *Chapter 5*

# From Seth and Cain to Noah, the Great Flood, and God's Chosen People

*Then Cain went away from the presence of the LORD and settled in the land of Nod, east of Eden. Cain knew his wife, and she conceived and bore Enoch. When he built a city, he called the name of the city after the name of his son, Enoch. — Genesis 4:16–17*

CAIN LEFT ADAM and Eve and settled in Nod. Importantly, the Bible notes Cain *went away from the presence of the Lord*, married *his wife*, and *built a city*. I have never heard a pastor or Bible teacher explain who Cain married, except one pastor who said Cain married his sister. No sister is mentioned in the Bible, and there would be no reason for a sister to be banished from her parents along with Cain. And why would Cain have built a city if no other people existed on Earth? And how did areas like Nod outside of Eden already have names if no one ever lived there?

The obvious answer to these questions is, there were tribes of early humans all around Eden. Why else would Cain have been afraid someone would kill him? These other tribes were well-developed societies where Cain taught the people to create and play musical instruments, forge metals, live in tents, and keep livestock.[1]

Scientists have theorized for decades early humans were animal-like, dumb savages. However, more recent studies are revealing early humans were much more advanced than once thought:

> Our surprising findings at Abric Pizarro show how adaptable Neanderthals were. . . . Stone tools and animal bones discovered by the researchers show how Neanderthals were highly adaptive creatures, busting the popular misconception that they were poor hunters and pretty dumb.[2]

Scientists have confirmed modern humans did not evolve from Neanderthals but crossbred with them. Modern humans were also fearful of early humans. Cain, for example, believed they would kill him.

> Contrary to popular belief, despite some cross-breeding, Neanderthals and us, Homo sapiens, are not the same and we did not evolve from Neanderthals. We shared Earth with these monsters and it may not have been particularly pleasant. Some modern theorizing suggests Homo sapiens were more like prey to Neanderthals than any type of relative.[3]

Scientists are still wrong about when this cross-breeding occurred. Most estimate around 40,000 to 50,000 years ago. The Bible says Cain married an early human less than 10,000 years ago. The discrepancy is likely caused by the impact of the Great Flood which completely rearranged the Earth's surface about 4,500 years ago. Archaeologists assume the layers of dirt and rock lying on top of their discoveries are evidence of age. However, the Flood reshuffled the sands of time and covered all of the Earth with many layers of mud and rock.

Adam and Eve had another son named Seth. After the birth of Seth, the Bible describes two divergent paths for the generations of Seth and Cain. The Bible depicts the generations of Cain as violent and vengeful. The generations of Seth, however, *called upon the name of the LORD*.[4]

In Genesis 5, the Bible details the generations following Adam and Seth. Interestingly, the first few verses in chapter 5 seem to be making a distinction between Adam (modern humans) and early humans. These verses mention Adam and then switch to *when God created man,* using the generic word for *mankind*. It says mankind was created male and female in the likeness of God, and God named them *man*, Hebrew for *mankind*. Then the account goes back to Adam and tells us Adam's son was created in his likeness. This may be the first distinction between the *sons of man* and the *sons of God*:

> This is the book of the generations of Adam. When God created man, he made him in the likeness of God. Male and female he created them, and he blessed them and named them Man when they were created. When Adam had lived 130 years, he fathered a son in his own likeness, after his image, and named him Seth. (Genesis 5:1–3)

The Bible outlines the generations from Adam to Noah over 1,600 years. Lifespans were generally over 900 years. The specificity of the ages when sons were born and their ages when they died has an obvious purpose. God wants us to know how many years passed from the time of Adam to the Great Flood.

The Bible does not outline all the generations of Cain. Instead, it refers to his offspring generically as *man*, using the Hebrew word for *mankind*. But the crossbreeding between Cain and early humans had obviously created a different kind of human. Cain's daughters were more beautiful, and the *sons of God* (fallen angels who became human) married them. The breeding between Cain's female descendants and the *sons of God* apparently created powerful human beings including giants (Nephilim). God was not pleased:

> When man began to multiply on the face of the land and daughters were born to them, the sons of God saw that the daughters of man were attractive. And they took as their wives any they chose. Then the LORD said, "My Spirit shall not abide in man forever, for he is flesh: his days shall be 120 years." The Nephilim were on the earth in those days, and also afterward, when the sons of God came in to the daughters of man and they bore children to them. These were the mighty men who were of old, the men of renown. (Genesis 6:1–4)

## The Great Flood

The entire human race was infected with the wickedness of Satan and his fallen angels whose every intention and thought was evil. God decided to wipe all humans and animals (apparently animals were also infected with evil) off the face of the earth—all humans except Noah, his wife, his three sons and their wives and all animals except for those Noah took into the ark:

> The Lord saw that the wickedness of man was great in the earth, and that every intention of the thoughts of his heart was only evil continually. And the Lord regretted that he had made man on the earth, and it grieved him to his heart. So the Lord said, "I will blot out man whom I have created from the face of the land, man and animals and creeping things and birds of the heavens, for I am sorry that I have made them." But Noah found favor in the eyes of the Lord. (Genesis 6:5–8)

God told Noah to build an ark larger than a football field. The boat took decades for Noah and his sons to complete. When they finished, God told Noah to take his family and two of every animal inside. God called and guided these animals to the ark. Then the massive layer of water vapor covering Earth since creation fell as heavy rain for forty days. The weight of this water crushed Earth's surface and pressured the water below the surface to *burst forth*:

> On that day all the fountains of the great deep burst forth, and the windows of the heavens were opened. And rain fell upon the earth forty days and forty nights. (Genesis 7:11–12)

The floodwaters covered the entire earth for five months. I believe Earth's surface was very different before the flood. There were mountains, but much smaller than we have today. There were many small seas, but nothing like the large oceans that now cover most of our planet.

There is much evidence suggesting that all of Earth's vegetation, animal, and human life were carried by the floodwaters deep below the surface into large caverns after the heavy rains crushed the surface. The massive volumes of fossil fuel that exist today deep below ground had to come from all the organic material swept away by the flood. Scientists peddle the preposterous theory that decomposing organic material seeped deep below the surface over millions of years. There is no way reservoirs of hundreds of millions of gallons of oil could have been created by slow seepage!

The heavy floodwaters also collapsed large areas of Earth's surface, creating deep depressions for floodwaters to gather. Huge volumes of water rushed from higher elevations, digging deep ravines and valleys as they traveled to fill the areas that are now our oceans. When Earth's surface collapsed in many places around the world, the areas that didn't collapse became our mountains. The tops of the mountains we see today may have been ground level before the flood.

The weather on Earth also changed dramatically after the flood. The loss of the water vapor canopy surrounding Earth created weather patterns like those we have today. The poles froze while the middle areas around the equator experienced hot temperatures. Large oceans, warm temperatures, and evaporation created clouds and rain. There were seasonal changes in temperatures all around the world.

## The Floodwaters Diminished Evil on Earth

We should consider how the Flood accomplished God's purpose of destroying evil in the world. Before the Flood, many of Satan's demons were living as human beings. Their bodies were mortal, but they could occupy new hosts before their bodies died. The Bible speaks of demons moving from one host to another. They apparently had to find new hosts or their spirits would be trapped in the abyss. For example, when Jesus was about to cast many demons out of a man next to the Sea of Galilee, the demons begged Him to allow them to enter a herd of nearby pigs:

> Jesus then asked him [the demoniac], "What is your name?" And he said, "Legion," for many demons had entered him. And they begged him not to command them to depart into the abyss. Now a large herd of pigs was feeding there on the hillside, and they begged him to let them enter these. So he gave them permission. Then the demons came out of the man and entered the pigs, and the herd rushed down the steep bank into the lake and drowned. (Luke 8:30–33)

The drowning of the pigs in water apparently prevented the demons from finding other hosts. The water must have trapped the demons in their dying hosts. When we consider the role of water in baptism—separating people from their sin and designating them as God's children—it is reasonable to believe the flood not only killed the physical bodies of all evil people on Earth but also trapped many of Satan's demons in the spiritual abyss. By drowning all humans and animals at once, there was nowhere else for the demons to go.

God's commands and His covenant with Noah after the Flood provide insights into one of God's purposes for animals and mankind on Earth. When God created the first creatures in the sea and of the air, He told them to *be fruitful and multiply* (Genesis 1:22). When He created the first humans, He said, "*Be fruitful and multiply*" (Genesis 1:28). When the animals departed the ark after the flood, God told them to "*be fruitful and multiply* (Genesis 8:17). And God three times told Noah and his sons to *be fruitful and multiply* (Genesis 9:1 and twice in 9:7). The quantity of animals and humans on Earth is clearly a priority for God.

## All Heavenly Beings Will Inhabit Physical Bodies

All living beings in the spiritual world will, at some point in time, inhabit physical bodies as part of the process of being born of water (physical) and blood (spiritual). Many generations of physical bodies are needed to provide passage through the physical world for all spiritual beings. The end of heaven and Earth will not occur until all have come through the physical world.

In Romans, Paul's reference *until the fullness of the Gentiles has come in* suggests there is a progression of God's people who must come in before the final salvation of Israel:

> Lest you be wise in your own sight, I do not want you to be unaware of this mystery, brothers: a partial hardening has come upon Israel,

> until the fullness of the Gentiles has come in. (Romans 11:25)

Jesus, speaking to His disciples before His crucifixion, tells them they are not of this world but they are like Him who came from another world. We all came from another world and are just passing through the physical world:

> I have given them your word, and the world has hated them because they are not of the world, just as I am not of the world. I do not ask that you take them out of the world, but that you keep them from the evil one. They are not of the world, just as I am not of the world. (John 17:14–16)

Noah's sons and daughters-in-law apparently carried the genes of both modern and early humans. Even today, most humans still have a small percentage of Neanderthal in their DNA.[5] Apparently, DNA for the Nephilim (giants) also continued in modern humans as evidenced by Goliath and other giants in the land of Israel when the Jews returned from Egypt.

## Shem Produces the Line of Christ

Noah's son Shem became the patriarch of the line to Abraham, the father of God's chosen people the Jews.

Abraham became the father of Isaac, who became the father of Jacob (God changed Jacob's name to Israel), who became the father of twelve sons, the patriarchs of the twelve tribes of Israel.

The Jews were God's representatives on Earth until the birth of Jesus. God used the Jews to show how He would protect and deliver His people when they obeyed Him. We also learned from the Jews what happens to God's people when they disobey. The lessons apply directly to the Christian church today. The Jews are the physical depiction of the spiritual journey of all God's people.

The Jews began in the land promised to Abraham, the land that is Israel today. This is analogous to all members of God's family beginning as spiritual beings in heaven. The Jews had to leave the Promised Land because of famine, but Joseph, one of Jacob's twelve sons, had been sold into slavery and taken to Egypt earlier. God used Joseph to save the family.

## Egypt Symbolizes the Physical World

Egypt is symbolic of the physical world. In the Bible, Egypt represents the world systems of power, wealth, and wickedness. It serves as both a place of refuge and protection as well as a place of enslavement and hardship. God used Joseph, a one-time slave in Egypt, to prepare a place to send Joseph's family and save them from famine. This is analogous to God sending Jesus into the world to save His people from sin. Perhaps the war in heaven created the need for God's people to leave and seek temporary refuge in the physical world. Or, more likely, God sent His people into the physical world in response to Satan's challenge that He give His people the freedom to choose good or evil.[6]

Jesus was born in the Promised Land but taken to Egypt for His protection from Herod who sent soldiers to Bethlehem to kill Him. This is the physical enactment of Satan being poised to *devour* the child from God in the book of Revelation.[7] God took the first incarnation of Jesus to heaven for His protection just as Jesus's parents took Him to Egypt for protection. Years later, Jesus and His family left Egypt and returned to the Promised Land to prepare for His ministry to save His people—just as the resurrected Jesus would one day leave Earth to prepare an eternal place for His people.

## The Jews Represent the Body of Christ

While in captivity, the Jews grew in numbers and essentially became a nation. God sent Moses to save His people from slavery. The whole process of Moses saving God's people is instructive for Christians today. The blood of a lamb on their doors in Egypt saved the Jews from death while they were slaves. God still saves

His people even before we know Him. We do nothing to deserve God's love:

> God shows his love for us in that while we were still sinners, Christ died for us. (Romans 5:8)

Jesus must fight Satan for the release of His people just as Moses had to contend with Pharaoh to release the Jews. This battle causes terrible suffering for the people on Earth just as the Egyptian people suffered greatly because of the battle between Pharaoh and Moses. And even after God saves us from sin, Satan still pursues us just as Pharaoh pursued the Jews after Moses took them into the desert. God led His people through the Red Sea on dry land just as God saves us through the blood of Jesus.

The Jews were saved from slavery but refused to trust God to protect them in the Promised Land, so they remained in limbo in the desert for forty years. Most of the generation of Jews who left Egypt died in the desert without ever entering the Promised Land. This is analogous to many of God's people who are saved from their sin by the blood of Jesus but never trust Jesus as their Savior and Lord during their physical lives. They live their lives in limbo between slavery and freedom and never know Jesus in this life. Hebrews describes it as not having the faith to enter God's Sabbath rest.[8]

The decision to accept Jesus as Savior and Lord is analogous to the Jews finally crossing the Jordan into the Promised Land. But after the Jews entered the Promised Land, they had to constantly fight enemies all around them. This is what happens when we accept Jesus as Savior: we enlist in the battle between good and evil. The decision to accept Christ puts us on the front lines of the battle against Satan and the evil all around us. And like God did for the Jews, when Christians obey Him, He will fight for us. When we disobey, we will be defeated.

The Jews in Israel were much like the body of Christ today, the Church. There was much good and much bad. Sometimes they remembered what God had done for them, but most of the time they forgot. Many of the Jews worshipped idols just as many Christians today worship worldly possessions and follow godless people. God wants to be our king but the Jews wanted a human king like other nations even though God warned them a king would be a curse. Some Christians today think we need to elect our king.

The nation of Israel was divided into twelve tribes and eventually became two nations with rival kings. God sent prophets to warn His people to remember His laws and repent, but their leaders continued to lead them astray. Christians today are divided into many denominations and sects with many false prophets as their leaders. The nation of Israel was destroyed and taken into captivity by its enemies just as the apostate church will be destroyed along with the world system of the Antichrist. But God will always save a remnant comprised of all the people who were loyal to Him before the creation of Earth.

Israel was living under the tyrannical rule of the Romans and the oppression of hypocritical religious Pharisees when God came to Earth as a human. Jesus, the physical image of God, was born in humility in a stable even though He was God's Son and "*the way, and the truth, and the life* for all who accept Him (John 14:6). Jesus revealed He was the only way to the Father, the only way to eternal life.

## *Chapter 6*

# Jesus: The Only Truth, the Only Way to God, and the Only Means to Eternal Life

*Jesus said to him [His disciple Thomas],*
*"I am the way, and the truth, and the life.*
*No one comes to the Father except through me."*
*—John 14:6*

TRUTH IS LIKE a puzzle: you must put the pieces together.

I once participated in a leadership development program where puzzles were used as a team-building exercise. Our class was divided into teams of four, and each team was given a puzzle. But there was a catch: all the box tops had been switched, so the puzzle pieces didn't match the picture on the cover.

Our team-building exercise deteriorated into chaos as every team struggled to arrange the pieces to match the images on their box top. Most of the teams were able to assemble small sections of the puzzle with a few matching pieces. One of the groups put together all the edge pieces to create a frame, but even this was unattainable for most groups because the pieces didn't resemble the images on the box tops.

The truth requires the right box top. We must know the whole truth before we can properly understand all its component parts. The Bible has many pieces: histories, prophecies, parables and allegories, poetry, wise proverbs, journals, firsthand accounts of events, and spiritual teachings. All of these are separately true, but their meaning cannot be completely understood until we know the whole truth.

Jesus is the whole truth: He is the picture on the box top. All the pieces in the Bible come together to create the image of Jesus. The pieces collectively create the image, but the pieces will not fit together until we know what the image looks like. Jesus shows us the finished picture and guides us as we put all the pieces of the Bible together to shape the whole truth.

If we study the Bible with the wrong image of Jesus in mind, we will never discover the truth. If we think of Jesus as only a good man, or a wise teacher, or a great example, or a person who lived such a good life He became a god, we will never discover the truth of the Bible. If we think Jesus is a prophet sent by God with a message to save everyone, we will still never know the truth.

The truth begins with the most important fact in the universe: Jesus is and has always been the eternal, almighty God! He didn't become God, and He wasn't created by God. He has been God forever. The Bible describes Jesus as *the Word*, and then says *the Word was God* from the beginning:

> In the beginning was the Word, and the Word was with God, and the Word was God. He was in the beginning with God. (John 1:1–2)

*The Word* is the spoken word and the written word of God. He (Jesus) is God's voice and His inspired written words (the Bible). He is the power who created the physical universe. He is the energy holding all things together. He is God who became Jesus the man. Paul described Jesus as God in Colossians 1:15–20:

> He is the image of the invisible God, the firstborn of all creation. For by him all things were created, in heaven and on earth, visible and invisible, whether thrones or dominions or

> rulers or authorities—all things were created through him and for him. And he is before all things, and in him all things hold together. And he is the head of the body, the church. He is the beginning, the firstborn from the dead, that in everything he might be preeminent. For in him all the fullness of God was pleased to dwell, and through him to reconcile to himself all things, whether on earth or in heaven, making peace by the blood of his cross.

God's Word became a physical person but was not a separate being from God any more than our own voices are separate from us. Even in the physical world, our words are part of us and essentially who we are. Most of what we accomplish in life is the result of our spoken or written words. It shouldn't be too hard to imagine our words becoming a human being and carrying out our will.

Comparing ourselves to God is always a stretch, but we are made in God's image so there are things we can learn about God from our own experiences. We all have a will that can be described as our central control —like the Godhead and God the Father. We all have written and spoken words and we all emit a spirit with the power to change the atmosphere in a room. Some people can light up a room when they walk in the door. Others . . . —not so much.

Our wills, words, and spirits are all one just as God is three Persons in one, but unlike God, we are not omnipotent, omnipresent, omnificent, and omniscient. And our words will never become a human being who saves all of God's people, but our words can be used by God to lead people to Jesus.

## The Blood of Jesus Is the Only Way to Eternal Life

Jesus is God in human form, but unlike any other human, He was conceived by the Spirit of God the Father and a human mother. Jesus's DNA is both God and human, both spiritual and physical. His blood is the only means for humans to be born of both water and the spirit, to be restored to God's family, and to become spiritual and physical beings made for eternity.

But how could Jesus be sinless when all humans are born with a sin nature? The answer is simple: the sin nature we all inherit is passed to us by our fathers. Men transmit the sin nature through their seed. All men and women inherit a sin nature except Jesus because He did not have a human father.

When we repent of our sins and ask Jesus to forgive our sins, we are essentially asking God to replace our sinful physical blood with Jesus's perfectly righteous spiritual and physical blood. No other human being has ever had blood like Jesus. This is why the blood of Jesus is so important and why Holy Communion depicts the drinking of Jesus's blood. His blood gives us access to eternity. It is our only ticket to the new heaven on a new Earth.

Our lives may continue in the physical world for a period after we give our lives to Jesus, but His blood reconnects us to our spirits in heaven and we become spiritually alive. We are born again. The blood of Jesus purifies us from all sin and makes our bodies a holy temple where God's Holy Spirit can live. Jesus fills us with His presence. We become part of His body. The indwelling of God's Holy Spirit confirms we are part of God's family and have eternal life with Jesus.

## Jesus Pays the Price for Our Sin

Why did Jesus have to die to save His people? Because the punishment for sin is death. God told Adam if he ate from the Tree of the Knowledge of Good and Evil, he would die.[1] God wasn't saying he would die physically. We don't know if Adam and Eve would have ever died physically if they had not chosen to know evil. God was speaking about spiritual death. When Adam ate the forbidden fruit and gained the knowledge of evil, he became spiritually dead. He was immediately separated from God and the spiritual world. Separation from God is the result of sin. All of Adam's descendants inherited his condition of sin.

In the book of Romans, Paul reinforced the price we all pay for sin. He also reminded us we don't have to pay that price ourselves. Jesus gives us the free gift of life by paying the price for our sin himself. Jesus did not have to die for His own sin. That's why He is the only one qualified to die for ours:

> The wages of sin is death, but the free gift of God is eternal life in Christ Jesus our Lord. (Romans 6:23)

I should note there was a second tree of importance in the Garden: the Tree of Life. This tree offered eternal life, but there is no record of Adam and Eve eating from this tree. Apparently Adam and Eve could have chosen to live forever, but they didn't. After their fall, Adam and Eve were banished from the garden and blocked from returning because God did not want them to eat from the Tree of Life and live forever in a state of sin (Genesis 3:24). The Tree of Life is mentioned again in Revelation in the description of the new heaven. It bears new fruit every month, and its leaves heal the nations (Revelation 22:2),

## God Justifies and Saves His People

Does God's gift of eternal life apply to everyone? I don't think so. In the Bible, God only rescues His people. Aren't we all God's people? No. Before the creation of the world, God chose those who will have eternal life.[2] When God sent Moses to Egypt, He sent him to save His physical people:

> "Come, I will send you to Pharaoh that you may bring my people, the children of Israel, out of Egypt." (Exodus 3:10)

Jesus said He came to save His sheep and only His sheep would recognize His voice and follow Him. The people who are not His do not know His voice and cannot believe because they are not His sheep:

> "I told you, and you do not believe. The works that I do in my Father's name bear witness about me, but you do not believe because you are not among my sheep. My sheep hear my voice, and I know them, and they follow me. I give them eternal life, and they will never perish, and no one will snatch them out of my hand. My Father, who has given them to me, is greater than all, and no one is able to snatch them out of the Father's hand. I and the Father are one." (John 10:25–30)

We can learn a lot about God's purposes, Jesus's role, and the proper response of God's people from the stories about the nation of Israel. Here are some of the parallels between the nation of Israel and the body of Christ, the Church.

| ***God's Chosen Physical People*** | ***God's Chosen Spiritual People*** |
|---|---|
| *The Nation of Israel* | *The Body of Christ: The Church* |
| Originated in the Promised Land as twelve tribes led by the sons of Jacob | Originated in heaven before the creation of the world |
| One son, Joseph, was sold into slavery and taken to Egypt. | God's Son, Jesus, was sent to the physical world as a servant to save His people. |
| Israel left the Promised Land because of famine and went to Egypt to save themselves. | All God's people must leave heaven and pass through the physical world to be saved. |
| The Jews became slaves in Egypt. | God's children became slaves to sin on Earth. |
| God sent Moses to free His people from slavery. | God sent Jesus to save His people from slavery to sin and death. |

| ***God's Chosen Physical People*** | ***God's Chosen Spiritual People*** |
|---|---|
| *The Nation of Israel* | *The Body of Christ: The Church* |
| Moses contended with Pharaoh to free God's people. | Jesus contended with Satan by resisting all his temptations. |
| The blood of a lamb on the doors of the Jews' homes saved them from death. | Jesus's blood saves all God's people from death. |
| Moses defeated Pharaoh and led Israel through the Red Sea to freedom in the desert. (The people did nothing to earn this freedom and quickly forgot how God saved them.) | Jesus's death (the shedding of blood) and His resurrection defeated Satan, saved all God's people from the eternal consequences of their sin, and gave them eternal life in heaven, (God's people do nothing to earn this gift, and many aren't yet aware they have been given eternal life.)Believers—as the Church—are constantly at war with Satan, the prince of this world. We defeat Satan when we obey God. |

The Jews did not trust God and refused to cross the Jordan into the Promised Land, so the entire generation of Jews who were freed from Egypt—except for Joshua and Caleb who trusted God—died in the desert.

During their physical lives, many of God's people who are justified by the blood of Jesus never trust God to save them. They do not cross over into God's promised rest through faith in Christ. They are saved for eternity but waste their lives separated from God in a spiritual desert.

Joshua convinced the Jews to trust God and led them through the Jordan River into the Promised Land.

Jesus sent His Holy Spirit to convict God's people of sin and call them to receive Jesus as Savior and Lord. Those who receive Jesus are resurrected to spiritual life, indwelt by the Holy Spirit, and immediately restored to God's presence. They enter God's promised rest during their physical lives.

God's people in the Promised Land were constantly at war with adversaries who occupied the land. They were victorious when they obeyed God.

Believers—as the Church—are constantly at war with Satan, the prince of this world. We defeat Satan when we obey God.

The stories about Israel suggest there are many people in this world who don't belong to God. Instead, Satan owns them. Jesus also said even religious leaders can be children of Satan. In the verse below, for instance, Jesus was speaking to the Pharisees, the most prominent religious leaders of the Jews:

> "You are of your father the devil, and your will is to do your father's desires. He was a murderer from the beginning, and does not stand in the truth, because there is no truth in him. When he lies, he speaks out of his own character, for he is a liar and the father of lies." (John 8:44)

## Two Stages of Salvation

Jesus saves His people from sin and gives us eternal life before we are born. In the opening of his letter to Titus, Paul referred to *eternal life, which God, who never lies, promised before the ages began* (Titus 1:2).

Our faith in this life is how we *take hold* of that eternal life:

> Fight the good fight of the faith. Take hold of the eternal life to which you were called and about which you made the good confession in

> the presence of many witnesses. (1 Timothy 6:12)

We do nothing in this life to deserve or earn eternal life. But we cannot know God, become spiritually alive, or experience the joy of our salvation during our physical lives until we are born again by repenting and giving our lives to Jesus. We cannot enter God's kingdom while we're on Earth until we are cleansed of sin and filled with God's Holy Spirit.

So, there are two types of salvation referenced in the Bible. God's people have salvation unto eternal life because Jesus paid the price for sin before we were born. This first salvation for eternal life is like the Jews going through the Red Sea into the desert. The second salvation requires faith in Jesus to take us across the Jordan into the Promised Land. This is when we accept Jesus as Savior and Lord.

We are not saved by what we believe; we are able to believe because we are saved. Satan and his demons believe in God and know Jesus very well. As James noted, *Even the demons believe—and shudder!* (James 2: 19), but they are not saved.

A legion of demons cried out to Jesus from a possessed man: They knew Jesus, believed in Him and feared Him, but they would never be saved."*What have you to do with me, Jesus, Son of the Most High God? I beg you, do not torment me*" (Luke 8:28

Hebrews 11 is all about faith and the patriarchs who believed God. Nowhere in this chapter did the writer suggest faith saves people for eternity. Instead, faith gives us the certainty of God's promises and assurance of our hope for eternal life:

> Now faith is the assurance of things hoped for, the conviction of things not seen. For by it the people of old received their commendation. (Hebrews 11:1)

Abraham's faith was counted as righteousness because it was authenticated by his obedience to God:

> By faith Abraham obeyed when he was called to go out to a place that he was to receive as an inheritance. And he went out, not knowing where he was going. (Hebrews 11:8)

Our belief in Jesus allows Him to heal our infirmities,[3] cleanse us of sin, fill us with His Holy Spirit, and reconnect us with our spiritual selves in the heavenly realm.[4] Our conviction of sin, our repentance, our genuine belief in Jesus as Savior, and our humble acceptance of Him as our Lord and God confirms our salvation for eternal life.

We do not earn eternal life with good works or by praying to receive Christ. These acts confirm we belong to God and have eternal life. Good works don't save us, but we are saved to do good works. Genuine faith produces righteousness and action.

> What good is it, my brothers, if someone says he has faith but does not have works? Can that faith save him? (James 2:14)

## God's Purpose for His People

God has many purposes for His people on Earth. Among those purposes, He wants us to know Him through His Son and to know we have eternal life:

> I write these things to you who believe in the name of the Son of God, that you may know that you have eternal life. (1 John 5:13)

God wants us to know He loves us and to share His love with others so the whole world will know we love Him:

> This is my commandment, that you love one another as I have loved you. (John 15:12)

Good works don't save us, but God saves us to do good works. And the best work we can do—the most important fruit we can bear—is to love each other:

> "You did not choose me, but I chose you and appointed you that you should go and bear fruit and that your fruit should abide, so that whatever you ask the Father in my name, he may give it to you. These things I command you, so that you will love one another." (John 15:16–17)

The highest purpose of God's people on Earth is to win the battle between good and evil. Satan challenged God to let His people know evil, suffering, and death. Satan claimed if God doesn't protect and bless His people, they will curse Him and choose to follow Satan.[5] When God's people obey Him, praise and worship Him, love each other, resist evil, and give our lives to Jesus, we weaken Satan and prove God right. This is how the body of Christ will eventually defeat Satan, prove Satan wrong, and justify God's salvation of His people. But disobedience by God's people empowers Satan.

When God's people don't know Jesus or they refuse to accept Him as Savior and Lord, Satan wins. When God's people disobey and continue to practice sin, Satan wins. When Satan wins, God's people suffer. Much of the suffering in the world is the result of God's people failing to obey God and allowing Satan to win.

This is why evangelism and discipleship are so important. We are recruiting an army of people who believe and obey God. God Himself doesn't fight evil in this world; His people do. The war that began in heaven continues on Earth, and the outcome of the war between good and evil depends on God's people just as the outcome of the war in heaven depended on God's angels to expel Satan.

## How Do We Know Who Are God's People?

God's people are all over the earth in every country and among every race and religion. Many, however, don't know the true God and follow false gods. Many are agnostic or even atheists. If you question whether those who don't know Jesus now can be God's people, think about this: there are millions of people all over the world from every religion who don't know Jesus now but who will accept Jesus as their Savior and Lord during their lives. That means they are God's chosen people now whether they know it or not.

But everyone in this world (including God's chosen people) who has the ability to choose between good and evil but is not following Jesus is following Satan. They are fighting on Satan's side in the war between good and evil. Without knowing it, they are promoting both evil and suffering in the world. They are helping

Satan advance evil even if they think they are doing good works.

God calls all His people to repentance, but not all will answer His call, just like the Jews who died in the desert because they didn't trust God to save them:

> Isaiah cries out concerning Israel: "Though the number of the sons of Israel be as the sand of the sea, only a remnant of them will be saved, for the Lord will carry out his sentence upon the earth fully and without delay." (Romans 9:27–28)

Many were saved from slavery in Egypt, but most did not have the faith to enter the Promised Land. The same is true for God's spiritual children. Many are saved from eternal death by the blood of Jesus, but by not accepting Jesus as Savior and Lord, they are not saved and made alive spiritually during their physical lives.

All people live, suffer, and die in the physical world to answer Satan's demands for freedom and justice. God's people, however, have the freedom to know good and evil, the opportunity to choose between God and Satan, and the ability to bring justice to Satan by obeying God and defeating evil.

Do some of God's chosen people still live and die in the desert without ever giving their lives to Jesus? I think so. I believe the blood and sacrifice of Jesus justified all God's people. His blood paid the price for our sins and gave us eternal life before we were born in this physical world. We do nothing to earn it, but we cannot know the peace of God and know we are saved until we give our lives to Jesus.

God's gift of salvation and eternal life applies to all His people, many who never know Him on Earth. This includes unborn children who are aborted, children who die before they have the ability to understand, the mentally disabled, and the many who never hear the good news of Jesus.

In summary, there are two aspects of salvation for God's chosen people. The first happens in the spiritual world before we are conceived as humans. That's when the blood of Jesus redeems us and gives us eternal life (eternal life is certain for God's people and has nothing to do with what we do during our lives on Earth). The second aspect of salvation can occur when we repent of our sin and accept Jesus as our Lord and Savior during our lives on Earth. This second step is our responsibility and requires willful action, and it is the only way we humans can be reconnected with God.

Before the creation of the world, God chose those who would be saved for eternity. This selection process may have been completely arbitrary with some people destined for eternal hell and some for eternal life. God certainly has the prerogative to do whatever

He chooses. But I think God allowed all His created beings to decide for themselves whether to choose God or Satan. This option is more consistent with God's character of perfect freedom.

I think the people doomed to hell before the creation of the world are physical images of the angels who rebelled against God and were thrown out of heaven. They all eventually become human beings and die physically, and their spirits will be thrown into a burning abyss for eternity. This destiny is fair and just because they chose to be separated from God and were determined to destroy God and His people.

God's people are physical images of the angels who chose to fight against Satan in the war in heaven. Their names were written into the book of life before they were born. When these people—past, present, and future— choose to follow Jesus during their physical lives, they rejoin the fight against Satan in the physical world.

The sacrifice of Jesus justifies all of God's people and saves them for eternal life in heaven. Just as the Jewish priests made sacrifices for all of God's people, Jesus sacrificed His life and shed His blood to redeem (to buy back) all of God's people. This first phase of salvation is analogous to the blood of a lamb spread on the doorframes of the Jewish homes in Egypt to save them from death. Then Moses led the Jewish people out of Egypt to freedom in the desert. The Jews were saved from death and slavery, but they were not yet in the Promised Land that represents God's kingdom.

Jesus's parable about the wedding feast tells us a lot about who and why God chooses certain people. In this parable, the king invites a large group of people to his son's wedding, but those he invites will not come. They refuse to come, and they kill the king's messengers. The king sends his army to kill them all. This is analogous to God inviting all His heavenly hosts to celebrate the marriage of His Son Jesus to His bride, the Church. Many refuse, fight against God, and are condemned to eternal death. These are the angels who refused God's invitation to life and started the war in heaven.

As Jesus observed, *Many are called, but few are chosen* (Matthew 22:14). God's chosen are like the undeserving guests who accepted the king's invitation. God redeems all His chosen by covering them with the blood of Jesus (wedding garments in the parable). But one of the guests did not have wedding garments, which means he was not covered by the blood of Jesus. He accepted the king's invitation but he was not one of God's chosen. So he was thrown out into the darkness.

God chooses His people for eternal salvation but God's people must choose to cross over from death to life if they are to be saved during their physical lives. We must put on wedding garments—the blood of

Jesus—to know God. We must cross the Jordan into the Promised Land. God decides who are His people, but His people will not know they are saved unless they make a conscious decision to repent and accept Jesus during their physical lives.

The Bible is clear: there is no spiritual life in this world and no eternal life unless we are covered by the blood of Jesus. Traditional interpretations hold that people must believe in Jesus during their physical lives to have eternal life:

> For God so loved the world, that he gave his only Son, that whoever believes in him should not perish but have eternal life. (John 3:16)

Other verses confirm only those who have Jesus have life:

> This is the testimony, that God gave us eternal life, and this life is in his Son. Whoever has the Son has life; whoever does not have the Son of God does not have life. (1 John 5:11–12)

This verse has two parts. (1) God gave us eternal life in Jesus and (2) only those who have the Son have life. John later referred to those who believe in Jesus as those who are "*born of God*."[6] Only those who believe in Jesus have eternal life. But John then said he wrote these things so people will know they have eternal life:

> I write these things to you who believe in the name of the Son of God, that you may know that you have eternal life. (1 John 5:13)

My conclusion: our ability to hear and believe the gospel of Jesus is confirmation we are already saved. Jesus told us in many places that only God's people *have ears to hear*[7] the Word. Our ability to believe and our acceptance of Jesus as Savior and Lord are not what gives us eternal life. Our belief and acceptance are instead evidence God has already saved us and given us eternal life after first giving us ears to hear. Even our faith is a gift from God.[8]

There have been millions of God's chosen people who have lived and died around the world without knowing or accepting Jesus. This includes the unborn and young children. They died without ever being born of God during their physical lives. But they were saved from sin and death by the work of Jesus because God chose them as His own before the creation of the world. Those who live their lives without repenting of their sins and accepting Jesus may do many good deeds, but it is all meaningless because their good works are not built on a solid foundation. They still have eternal life, but they will receive no reward for their time on Earth:

> If the work that anyone has built on the foundation survives, he will receive a reward. If anyone's work is burned up, he will suffer loss, though he himself will be saved, but only as through fire. (1 Corinthians 3:14–15)

Just as there are many who have been given eternal life but never know Jesus during their physical lives, there are also many who—like the man in the parable of the wedding feast who didn't have wedding garments—think they are saved but are not actually part of God's family. Jesus said many will come to Him on judgment day who are not His, and He will turn them away:

> "Not everyone who says to me, 'Lord, Lord,' will enter the kingdom of heaven, but the one who does the will of my Father who is in heaven. On that day many will say to me, 'Lord, Lord, did we not prophesy in your name, and cast out demons in your name, and do many mighty works in your name?' And then will I declare to them, 'I never knew you; depart from me, you workers of lawlessness.'" (Matthew 7:21–23)

The people in these verses are religious people who are claiming their good works, done in the name of Christ, should save them. They believe in Jesus, but their faith is not genuine because they do not have the ability to hear the truth and believe. They are not God's chosen people.

A part of the verse above says, *But [only] the one who does the will of my Father* will enter the kingdom of heaven. Isn't the will of the Father for all His people to come to Jesus? Yes, but God's will cannot be fulfilled in this evil world except to the degree God's people make it happen. Jesus told us to pray for God's will to be done on Earth as it is in heaven, but that prayer will only become reality in the new heaven on a new Earth.

It is very difficult for us to know who God's people are in this life. Many apparently good and religious people belong to Satan. Many bad people belong to God but don't yet know Jesus. Many of God's people who have accepted Jesus continue in their sinful lives (this may be a sign they are not really God's people).

Since we cannot know for sure who God's people are or who is able to receive the gospel message, we must present Jesus to everyone. Those who have ears to hear have the ability to respond: some will respond and some won't. The Bible tells us to love everyone including our enemies because we don't know who are our brothers and sisters in Jesus.

## How Do You Know If You Have Eternal Life?

How do you know if you are one of God's chosen? How do you know if you have eternal life? There are many ways to confirm your salvation:

- Have you humbled yourself, admitted you are a sinner, committed to turn from your sin with God's help, and asked Jesus to take control of your life?
- Has your decision to accept Jesus changed your life? Are you moving away from *works of the flesh* and exhibiting more of the *fruit of the Spirit*?

> Now the works of the flesh are evident: sexual immorality, impurity, sensuality, idolatry, sorcery, enmity, strife, jealousy, fits of anger, rivalries, dissensions, divisions, envy, drunkenness, orgies, and things like these. I warn you, as I warned you before, that those who do such things will not inherit the kingdom of God. But the fruit of the Spirit is love, joy, peace, patience, kindness, goodness, faithfulness, gentleness, self-control; against such things there is no law. And those who belong to Christ Jesus have crucified the flesh with its passions and desires. (Galatians 5:19–24)

- Do you love others as yourself, especially your brothers and sisters in Jesus?[9]
- Has the Bible come alive to you? Are you seeking to know and understand more of what it says?
- Do you have a sense of peace in your life despite troubles and hardship? Do you really trust God to make all things work for good (Romans 8:28)?

God wants us to know we have eternal life. He wants us to know His love. If we truly seek Him, we are His. God wants us to fulfill His purpose during our physical lives. He wants us to choose good, prove Satan wrong, and help win the battle between good and evil. It sounds overwhelming, but we can do all things through Christ who strengthens us.[10]

Jesus is the whole Truth and nothing but the Truth (John 14:6). The better we understand the Bible, the clearer we will see Jesus. And the clearer we see Jesus, the more we will understand the Bible.

## *Chapter 7*

# The Real Meaning of the Book of Revelation

TRADITIONAL TEACHINGS ABOUT Revelation present the book as a prediction of what will happen from the time of Christ's resurrection until His return at the end of time. But that's only part of what it really says. Revelation reveals the history of the world from both the spiritual and the physical perspectives, including the introduction of the world system, the first incarnation of Jesus, the war in heaven, Satan being thrown out of heaven and down to Earth, the mass destruction of the original creation, the Garden of Eden, and the continuous battle between good and evil.

The whole picture of Revelation is essential to understanding what the Bible really says, especially in Genesis. In the mysterious presentations in Revelation, we can see what Genesis really says about the world before the creation of modern humans, why the Garden of Eden was necessary, and how modern humans became the line of Christ. A fresh look at Revelation also reveals the signs of the end times now occurring all around us.

Revelation is complicated, but it is easier to grasp once we realize it includes the history of civilizations on Earth long before Adam and Eve were created. Revelation makes no sense if we try to interpret it only as predictions of future events.

The book of Revelation begins with a statement of its purpose: to tell the followers of Jesus what will happen before He returns. God the Father gave this revelation to Jesus who then gave it to an angel who gave it to the apostle John, one of the twelve disciples of Jesus. John wrote Revelation while he was in prison on the island of Patmos for preaching the gospel of Jesus:

> The revelation of Jesus Christ, which God gave him to show to his servants the things that must soon take place. He made it known by sending his angel to his servant John, who bore witness to the word of God and to the testimony of Jesus Christ, even to all that he saw. (Revelation 1:1–2)

John wrote that he was *in the spirit on the Lord's day* when he heard a loud voice behind him (Revelation 1:10). John turned to see Jesus in a glorified body standing among lampstands representing the seven churches. Jesus was standing symbolically among all His followers, all of the Church.

John was told to write down what he saw in two parts: *those [things] that are and those [things] that are to take place after this.* The things that are include the sum of everything that has come before. When we use the expression, "That's just the way things are," we are implicitly recognizing that the current situation is the sum total of everything that happened in the past.

> Write therefore the things that you have seen, those that are and those that are to take place after this. (Revelation 1:19)

Jesus told John to write down what he saw and send it to the seven churches:

> Write what you see in a book and send it to the seven churches, to Ephesus and to Smyrna and to Pergamum and to Thyatira and to Sardis and to Philadelphia and to Laodicea. (Revelation 1:11)

The seven churches were real churches when the book of Revelation was written, but the messages are directed at all followers of Jesus today and to all God's children who are not yet following Jesus but who have ears to hear the message.

| ***Message to Seven Churches*** | ***Message to All Christians*** |
|---|---|
| ***To the Church in Ephesus:*** | |
| Commendation: *I know your works, your toil and your patient endurance, and how you cannot bear with those who are evil.* (Revelation 2:2) | Christians are commended for hard work, patience amid hardship, and impatience with evil people. |
| Warning: *But I have this against you, that you have abandoned the love you had at first.* (Revelation 2:4) | The worries of life often distract Christians and turn us from our initial excitement and love for Jesus. |
| Challenge and Reward: *He who has an ear, let him hear what the Spirit says to the churches. To the one who conquers I will grant to eat of the tree of life, which is in the paradise of God.* (Revelation 2:7) | Only God's chosen people can hear His call and admonitions. He challenges us to listen, to act, and to be victorious against evil. The reward is eternal life. |
| ***To the Church in Smyrna:*** | |
| Commendation: *I know your tribulation and your poverty (but you are rich) and the slander of those who say that they are Jews and are not, but are a synagogue of Satan.* (Revelation 2:9) | God knows we will suffer in this life, but He tells us we are rich in Jesus. He reminds us we live among people who call themselves Jews and Christians but are really the children of Satan. |

| | |
|---|---|
| Warning: *Do not fear what you are about to suffer. Behold, the devil is about to throw some of you into prison, that you may be tested.* (Revelation 2:10) | God tells us not to fear when we are attacked by Satan. |
| Challenge and Reward: *Be faithful unto death, and I will give you the crown of life. He who has an ear, let him hear what the Spirit says to the churches.* (Revelation 2:10–12) | God expects us to be faithful until death, not necessarily to win every battle in this life. He will give to the faithful the crown of life. If you can hear His message, you are His and have eternal life through Jesus. |

***To the Church in Pergamum:***

| | |
|---|---|
| Commendation: *I know where you dwell, where Satan's throne is. Yet you hold fast my name, and you did not deny my faith.* (Revelation 2:13) | God knows where we live: in Satan's world. He commends us for staying faithful to Him even when fellow Christians suffer and are killed for standing up for Jesus. |
| Warning: *But I have a few things against you: you have some there who hold the teaching of Balaam, who taught Balak to put a stumbling block before the sons of Israel, so that they might eat food sacrificed to idols and practice sexual immorality. So also you have some who hold the teaching of the Nicolaitans. Therefore repent."* (Revelation 2:14) | Christians will increasingly be faced with false teachings even within many churches. Many churches already accept and celebrate forms of sexual immorality the Bible clearly says are wrong. We must repent for accepting wrong teaching. |

| Message to Seven Churches | Message to All Christians |
|---|---|
| ***To the Church in Pergamum* continued:** | |
| Challenge and Reward: *He who has an ear, let him hear what the Spirit says to the churches. To the one who conquers I will give some of the hidden manna, and I will give him a white stone, with a new name written on the stone that no one knows except the one who receives it.* (Revelation 2:17) | God is challenging His people to hear what the Spirit says and to overcome all the challenges we face. He promises rewards we can't even imagine. |
| ***To the Church in Thyatira:*** | |
| Commendation: *I know your works, your love and faith and service and patient endurance, and that your latter works exceed the first.* (Revelation 2:19) | God is worshipped and praised when we do good works, love others, keep our faith, and especially when we increase in faithfulness over time. |
| Warning: *But I have this against you, that you tolerate that woman Jezebel, who calls herself a prophetess and is teaching and seducing my servants to practice sexual immorality and to eat food sacrificed to idols.* (Revelation 2:20) | Many Christians have been conditioned to accept sexual immorality even among pastors and church leaders. |

| | |
|---|---|
| Challenge and Reward: *Only hold fast what you have until I come. The one who conquers and who keeps my works until the end, to him I will give authority over the nations, and he will rule them with a rod of iron, as when earthen pots are broken in pieces, even as I myself have received authority from my Father. And I will give him the morning star. He who has an ear, let him hear what the Spirit says to the churches.* (Revelation 2:25–29) | God tells His people to hold fast and conquer. He expects us to fight against evil. He will reward the faithful with authority over nations. All these messages to the churches are to those who have an ear to hear, to those who truly are God's people. |

***To the Church in Sardis:***

| | |
|---|---|
| Commendation: *I know your works. You have the reputation of being alive, but you are dead.* (Revelation 3:1) There is no commendation for this church. | Many people in Christian churches appear religious, but do not know Jesus. They are spiritually dead and separated from God. |
| Warning: *Wake up, and strengthen what remains and is about to die, for I have not found your works complete in the sight of my God.* (Revelation 3:2) | God expects good deeds—righteous service—from His people. Faith without good works is dead. |

| ***Message to Seven Churches*** | ***Message to All Christians*** |
|---|---|
| ***To the Church in Sardis* continued*:*** | |
| Challenge and Rewards: *Yet you have still a few names in Sardis, people who have not soiled their garments, and they will walk with me in white, for they are worthy. The one who conquers will be clothed thus in white garments, and I will never blot his name out of the book of life.* (Revelation 3:4–5) | Christians who continue in willful sin are likely not Christians at all. Those who confess their sin, repent, and then resist sin in their lives are listed in the book of life. |
| ***To the Church in Philadelphia:*** | |
| Commendation: *I know that you have but little power, and yet you have kept my word and have not denied my name.* (Revelation 3:8) | God loves the powerless who stand strong against the powerful forces of evil. Those who keep His Word and don't deny Jesus as Savior and Lord are commended by God. |
| Warnings: There is nothing negative said about this church. | |

| | |
|---|---|
| Challenge and Rewards: *Behold, I will make those of the synagogue of Satan who say that they are Jews and are not, but lie—behold, I will make them come and bow down before your feet, and they will learn that I have loved you. Because you have kept my word about patient endurance, I will keep you from the hour of trial that is coming on the whole world, to try those who dwell on the earth. I am coming soon. Hold fast what you have, so that no one may seize your crown. The one who conquers, I will make him a pillar in the temple of my God.* (Revelation 3:9–12) | God is warning us there will be many who call themselves Christians but are not. They are of the church of Satan. These false Christians will eventually be judged by the faithful who are powerless in this life. |

***To the Church in Laodicea:***

| | |
|---|---|
| Commendation: There is no commendation for this church. | |
| Warnings: *I know your works: you are neither cold nor hot. Would that you were either cold or hot! So, because you are lukewarm, and neither hot nor cold, I will spit you out of my mouth.* (Revelation 3:15–16) | This warning describes many Christian churches in the world today. People go to church on Sundays as part of their weekly routine, but it means very little to them. There is no passion in their worship and no dedication to serve God. |

| Message to Seven Churches | Message to All Christians |
|---|---|
| ***To the Church in Laodicea* continued:** | |
| Challenge and Rewards: *Those whom I love, I reprove and discipline, so be zealous and repent. Behold, I stand at the door and knock. If anyone hears my voice and opens the door, I will come in to him and eat with him, and he with me. The one who conquers, I will grant him to sit with me on my throne, as I also conquered and sat down with my Father on his throne.* (Revelation 3:19–21) | Jesus is speaking to God's children who have never repented and given their lives to Him. He says He is at the door of our hearts and knocking. He is inviting all His people to open the door so we can come join Him on the throne of God. This is an open invitation to all God's people who have ears to hear. |

The book of Revelation is written for faithful followers of Jesus, for believers in Jesus who have fallen away from true faith, and for all of God's people who have not repented and given their lives to Jesus. It is the complete and final revelation from God given to mankind.

## How to Understand Revelation

Revelation is unlike any other book in the Bible. It is unlike any book you've ever read. It is not describing events in chronological order. It jumps from scenes in the spiritual world to scenes in the physical world. And intermittingly, it repeats summaries outlining thousands of years of history in a few paragraphs.

John was brought into the spiritual world where he saw dozens of vignettes all around him like a crib mobile spinning above a baby. John looked and saw different things that have happened and will happen in both the physical and the spiritual worlds. John was seeing everything in a timeless spiritual world. Many of the events John saw were past events that created the stage for the things that would happen after John wrote Revelation. John saw the past and the future all at once.

The context of future events is established by all that has come before. The entire history as well as the future of the world is contained in the first scroll that had writing on both sides. Two-sided scrolls were rare when John wrote Revelation. This unusual scroll contained on one side accounts of events that occur in the physical world and, on the other side, events that occur in the spiritual world. The little scroll which is introduced later represents the much shorter period of time from the creation of Adam until the end of time. The events in the little scroll overlap the events in the seventh seal of the first scroll.

John began *in the spirit* on Earth but then saw an open door in heaven. Jesus told him to *"Come up here."* John found himself in a throne room with God the Father on the throne. The scene described by John begins with a depiction of heaven—past, present, and future. Revelation can only be understood if we try to grasp the concept of timelessness in the spiritual world. Everything that has happened and will happen in the physical world all happened in the present in the spiritual world. In that world there is no passage of time as we know it in the physical world.

The first scene John described in heaven is the preparation for everything in the spiritual world to be transported through the physical world. Events described in the past tense, such as the lamb sacrificed and believers put to death, were established in the spiritual world before the beginning of time.

I should note the numbers used in Revelation are often symbolic and significant. The number seven is used to signify complete and holy spiritual things. The numbers of four, six, twelve, and twenty-four represent things in the physical world. The number 666 is representative of the beast, which is the godless world system known in modern times as socialism and communism. The use of 1,000 years likely represents a long period of time and may not be a precise number of years.

In this first scene, we see twenty-four smaller thrones around the throne of God. These represent what will become the twelve tribes of Israel (the physical people of God) and the twelve disciples (the spiritual people of God: the Church of Jesus Christ). We also see four living creatures that represent different types of spiritual beings who will become living physical beings. Each of the living creatures is covered with eyes representing billions of individual physical beings. These living creatures have six wings indicating they will be traveling through the physical world.

The four living creatures represent the categories of physical beings created in Genesis 1. The lion represents the wild animals, the ox represents domesticated animals, the face of a man represents early humans, and the eagle represents the birds and the fish. All these heavenly beings are constantly praising God.

## The Scroll of World History and the Little Scroll of Modern History

There are two scrolls mentioned in Revelation that together present three story lines: two story lines from the scroll with seven seals and writing on both sides (the physical world on one side and the spiritual world on the other) and another story line from the little scroll containing events in the period from Adam to the resurrection of Jesus and then to the return of Jesus. There is a lot of overlap and repetition of these story lines. The chart below shows the overlap of events and attempts to put them in chronological order. The first side of the main scroll is a view from heaven where events are staged and initiated. The second side of the main scroll describe corresponding events on Earth. The little scroll is all about what happens on Earth after Adam.

The content of the first six seals describes events in heaven and Earth that happened before the creation of Adam and Eve during the period of God's rest. The destructive events on Earth outlined in the table below occurred between Genesis 2:4 and 2:5.

| ***Overview of the first side of the scroll: the spiritual perspective of what will happen on Earth*** | ***The meaning of writings from both sides of the scroll and the little scroll*** | ***Corresponding second side of the scroll and the little scroll: the physical outcome on Earth*** |
|---|---|---|
| First Seal: *And I looked, and behold, a white horse! And its rider had a bow, and a crown was given to him, and he came out conquering, and to conquer.* (Revelation 6:2) | This is Jesus the righteous King, the firstborn in all creation. His role is to fight and conquer the world system and make it God's kingdom. He is firstborn on Earth, but taken back to heaven for protection. Jesus appeared briefly as a man several times in the Old Testament (i.e., He was in the Garden of Eden, and He wrestled with Jacob), and then He was born as a child of Mary. | Satan attempted to stop God from establishing His kingdom on Earth by trying to kill His Son: *The dragon stood before the woman who was about to give birth, so that when she bore her child he might devour it. She gave birth to a male child, one who is to rule all the nations with a rod of iron, but her child was caught up to God and to his throne.* (Revelation 12:4–5) |

| ***Overview of the first side of the scroll: the spiritual perspective of what will happen on Earth*** | ***The meaning of writings from both sides of the scroll and the little scroll*** | ***Corresponding second side of the scroll and the little scroll: the physical outcome on Earth*** |
|---|---|---|
| Second Seal: *And out came another horse, bright red. Its rider was permitted to take peace from the earth, so that people should slay one another, and he was given a great sword.* (Revelation 6:4) | This is Satan the evil one who was *permitted to take peace from* God's perfect creation. He is the opponent of Jesus and the enemy of all God's people. | Satan's rebellion caused a war in heaven. He was defeated and thrown down to Earth: *Now war arose in heaven, Michael and his angels fighting against the dragon. And the dragon and his angels fought back, but he was defeated, and there was no longer any place for them in heaven. And the great dragon was thrown down, that ancient serpent, who is called the devil and Satan, the deceiver of the whole world—he was thrown down to the earth, and his angels were thrown down with him.* (Revelation 12:7–9) |

| | | |
|---|---|---|
| Third Seal: *And I looked, and behold, a black horse! And its rider had a pair of scales in his hand. And I heard what seemed to be a voice in the midst of the four living creatures, saying, "A quart of wheat for a denarius, and three quarts of barley for a denarius, and do not harm the oil and wine!"* (Revelation 6:5–6) | These references to money and commerce point to the world's political, economic, and religious systems. Jesus told us money is the root of all kinds of evil, represented here by a black horse. | The world system on Earth is represented by the two beasts. The first beast symbolizes the political and economic systems: *I saw a beast rising out of the sea, with ten horns and seven heads, with ten diadems on its horns and blasphemous names on its heads.* (Revelation 13:1)<br><br>The second beast represents the world's idolatrous religious systems: *Then I saw another beast rising out of the earth. It had two horns like a lamb and it spoke like a dragon.* (Revelation 13:11) |

| ***Overview of the first side of the scroll: the spiritual perspective of what will happen on Earth*** | ***The meaning of writings from both sides of the scroll and the little scroll*** | ***Corresponding second side of the scroll and the little scroll: the physical outcome on Earth*** |
|---|---|---|
| Fourth Seal: *I looked, and behold, a pale horse! And its rider's name was Death, and Hades followed him. And they were given authority over a fourth of the earth, to kill with sword and with famine and with pestilence and by wild beasts of the earth.* (Revelation 6:8) | This *rider* represents Satan and his demons who have the authority to use violence, famine, and disease to kill a fourth of the people on Earth. This explains why God's people face so much suffering and death on Earth. | Satan and his demons hit Earth with great force and destruction: *Another sign appeared in heaven: behold, a great red dragon, with seven heads and ten horns, and on his heads seven diadems. His tail swept down a third of the stars of heaven and cast them to the earth.* (Revelation 12:3–4) |
| Fifth Seal: *I saw under the altar the souls of those who had been slain for the word of God and for the witness they had borne.* (Revelation 6:9) | These were early humans killed by Satan and his demons. These humans are now waiting in heaven to be resurrected for eternity. | |

Sixth Seal: *There was a great earthquake, and the sun became black as sackcloth, the full moon became like blood, and the stars of the sky fell to the earth as the fig tree sheds its winter fruit when shaken by a gale. The sky vanished like a scroll that is being rolled up, and every mountain and island was removed from its place. Then the kings of the earth and the great ones and the generals and the rich and the powerful, and everyone, slave and free, hid themselves in the caves and among the rocks of the mountains, calling to the mountains and rocks, "Fall on us and hide us from the face of*

**In this account from the second side of the sixth seal, the seven trumpets announce the casting down of Satan and the destruction of Earth before Adam and Eve.**

This account tells of when Satan was thrown down to Earth before the creation of Adam and Eve. Satan is the *great star* that burns and poisons much of the earth. The whole world becomes a fiery wasteland.

*The first angel blew his trumpet and there followed hail and fire, mixed with blood, and these were thrown upon the earth. And a third of the earth was burned up, and a third of the trees were burned up, and all green grass was burned up.* (Revelation 8:7)

*The second angel blew his trumpet, and something like a great mountain, burning with fire, was thrown into the sea, and a third of the sea became blood. A third of the living creatures in the sea died, and a third of the ships were destroyed.* (Revelation 8:8–9)

| ***Overview of the first side of the scroll: the spiritual perspective of what will happen on Earth*** | ***The meaning of writings from both sides of the scroll and the little scroll*** | ***Corresponding second side of the scroll and the little scroll: the physical outcome on Earth*** |
|---|---|---|
| Sixth Seal: *continued*<br><br>*him who is seated on the throne, and from the wrath of the Lamb, for the great day of their wrath has come, and who can stand?"* (Revelation 6:12–17) | The *great star* is Satan. | *The third angel blew his trumpet, and a great star fell from heaven, blazing like a torch, and it fell on a third of the rivers and on the springs of water.* Revelation 8:10<br><br>*The fourth angel blew his trumpet, and a third of the sun was struck, and a third of the moon, and a third of the stars, so that a third of their light might be darkened, and a third of the day might be kept from shining, and likewise a third of the night.* (Revelation 8:12) |

| | | |
|---|---|---|
| Sixth Seal: *continued* | | *The fifth angel blew his trumpet, and I saw a star fallen from heaven to earth, and he was given the key to the shaft of the bottomless pit.* (Revelation 9:1)<br><br>*Then the sixth angel blew his trumpet, and I heard a voice from the four horns of the golden altar before God, saying to the sixth angel who had the trumpet, "Release the four angels who are bound at the great river Euphrates." So the four angels, who had been prepared for the hour, the day, the month, and the year, were released to kill a third of mankind. (Revelation 9:13–15)* |

| *Overview of the first side of the scroll: the spiritual perspective of what will happen on Earth* | *The meaning of writings from both sides of the scroll and the little scroll* | *Corresponding second side of the scroll and the little scroll: the physical outcome on Earth* |
|---|---|---|
| | After the destruction and death caused by Satan and his demons, all surviving humans were consumed with evil.<br><br>Many years passed on Earth with Satan and his demons possessing humans and animals and filling the world with evil. But God began to implement His plan to redeem the earth when He created modern humans as the line of the Savior. | *The rest of mankind, who were not killed by these plagues, did not repent of the works of their hands nor give up worshiping demons and idols of gold and silver and bronze and stone and wood, which cannot see or hear or walk, nor did they repent of their murders or their sorceries or their sexual immorality or their thefts.* (Revelation 9:20–21) |

***The Little Scroll***

The little scroll represents the history and the future of God's people on Earth from Adam and Eve until the end of time. John was told to eat the scroll which is symbolic of his consuming the contents so he could prophesy. He was told he must prophesy about another group of people: *I was told, "You must again prophesy about many peoples and nations and languages and kings."* (Revelation 10:11)

| | | |
|---|---|---|
| After the destruction Satan caused on Earth, God prepared to send His *sealed* people to Earth as modern humans: *And I heard the number of the sealed, 144,000, sealed from every tribe of the sons of Israel.* (Revelation 7:4) | God prepares to send His chosen physical and spiritual people to Earth, represented by the 144,000 in heaven who will become the two witnesses on Earth. | The little scroll describes two witnesses that represent Israel (olive trees) and the Church (lampstands), God's physical and spiritual people, respectively. These witnesses *shut the sky* like the prophet Elijah did, turned rivers into blood, created plagues like Moses, and were oppressed like God's people today. And we have seen what happens when enemies hurt Israel: *If anyone would harm them, fire pours from their mouth and consumes their foes.* (Revelation 11:5) |
| *These have been redeemed from mankind as firstfruits for God and the Lamb, and in their mouth no lie was found, for they are blameless.* (Revelation 14 4–5) | The 144,000 represent all of God's people who have lived and died on Earth, who have been redeemed and cleansed from all sin, and who now follow the resurrected Jesus in heaven waiting to return with Him. | |

| *Overview of the first side of the scroll: the spiritual perspective of what will happen on Earth* | *The meaning of writings from both sides of the scroll and the little scroll* | *Corresponding second side of the scroll and the little scroll: the physical outcome on Earth* |
|---|---|---|
| All God's spiritual people who have passed through the physical world return to heaven to celebrate around God's throne: *After this I looked, and behold, a great multitude that no one could number, from every nation, from all tribes and peoples and languages, standing before the throne and before the Lamb, clothed in white robes, with palm branches in their hands, and crying out with a loud voice, "Salvation belongs to our God who sits on the throne, and to the Lamb!"* (Revelation 7:9–10) | | The world persecutes and kills Jews and Christians, and the world system will eventually kill the Judeo-Christian biblical values around the world. But when all seems lost, God will rapture His people before the destruction of the world. *Then they heard a loud voice from heaven saying to them, "Come up here!" And they went up to heaven in a cloud, and their enemies watched them.* (Revelation 11:12) |

| | **The Seventh Trumpet** |
|---|---|
| On the second side of the scroll, the account of the seventh trumpet provides a review of the history of the world. It begins with the creation of Earth and the celebration in heaven because the world will become the kingdom of Christ: *Then the seventh angel blew his trumpet, and there were loud voices in heaven, saying, "The kingdom of the world has become the kingdom of our Lord and of his Christ, and he shall reign forever and ever."* (Revelation 11:15) | After the seventh trumpet, Revelation 12 and 13 take us back to the beginning and give a review of the second side of the large scroll. These events are described above and correspond to the opening of the first six seals in heaven. The second side of the scroll reveals what has happened on Earth since the beginning of the time. |

## The Great Flood Revealed in Revelation

After Satan was thrown down to Earth, he continued to pursue Adam, all his offspring, and the offspring of the woman who birthed Jesus. Revelation says Satan tried to destroy the line of Christ with a flood. Ironically, it appears that Satan tried to use the Great Flood described in Genesis to destroy God's people, but God used the flood to save a remnant of His people while Satan's people were destroyed. The water drained into Earth, and dry land reappeared. God often uses Satan's evil intentions for His own purposes:

> When the dragon saw that he had been thrown down to the earth, he pursued the woman who had given birth to the male child. But the woman was given the two wings of the great eagle so that she might fly from the serpent into the wilderness, to the place where she is to be nourished for a time, and times, and half a time. The serpent poured water like a river out of his mouth after the woman, to sweep her away with a flood. But the earth came to the help of the woman, and the earth opened its mouth and swallowed the river that the dragon had poured from his mouth. (Revelation 12:13–16)

## The Last Days of the Seventh Trumpet

We are currently living in the time after the seventh trumpet has blown. The seventh trumpet announced the countdown from the resurrection of Jesus until He returns to establish His kingdom on a new Earth. John saw a celebration in heaven and the preparation for the *marriage supper of the Lamb* when Jesus is reunited with His people (Revelation 19:9).

## The Rider on the White Horse: Jesus

After watching the celebration in heaven and the preparation of the marriage supper, John saw the rider—Jesus—on the white horse that was first introduced in Revelation 6. This section of Revelation has been misunderstood for centuries.

Traditionalists have interpreted the passages beginning at 19:11 as Jesus returning at the end of time, defeating Satan, and locking him in the bottomless pit for a thousand years. Jesus then establishes His kingdom on Earth for a thousand years before Satan is released to deceive the world and organize all the nations of the world to attack Israel where Jesus reigns.

This is an implausible scenario, and it is not what the passage means. How could Jesus reign on Earth for a thousand years among evil people and nations who all turn against Him? This is not what the Bible really says.

In Revelation 6 when the first seal of the two-sided scroll was opened, John described four horsemen. Jesus is the first horseman because He is first in all creation:

> Now I watched when the Lamb opened one of the seven seals, and I heard one of the four living creatures say with a voice like thunder, "Come!" And I looked, and behold, a white horse! And its rider had a bow, and a crown was given to him, and he came out conquering, and to conquer. (Revelation 6:1–2)

The four horsemen symbolize the four major forces operating in the world: Jesus and His people; Satan; Satan's people; and the world's political, economic, and religious systems. Jesus is introduced as the king who will fight and conquer the world system, represented by the first and second beasts in Revelation.

When John saw the rider of the white horse again in chapter 19, Jesus has died (*He is clothed in a robe dipped in blood* [verse 13]), has risen from the dead, and is preparing His return to establish His kingdom on Earth. This scene happens in heaven, not on Earth:

> Then I saw heaven opened, and behold, a white horse! The one sitting on it is called Faithful and True, and in righteousness he

> judges and makes war. His eyes are like a flame of fire, and on his head are many diadems, and he has a name written that no one knows but himself. He is clothed in a robe dipped in blood, and the name by which he is called is The Word of God. And the armies of heaven, arrayed in fine linen, white and pure, were following him on white horses. (Revelation 19:11–14)

After John saw Jesus on a white horse preparing to return, he saw the destruction of the beast and the leaders of the coalition of nations that had destroyed Babylon and are now attacking the followers of Jesus:

> I saw the beast and the kings of the earth with their armies gathered to make war against him who was sitting on the horse and against his army. And the beast was captured, and with it the false prophet who in its presence had done the signs by which he deceived those who had received the mark of the beast and those who worshiped its image. These two were thrown alive into the lake of fire that burns with sulfur. (Revelation 19:19–20)

John saw this same battle with the same result in another scene in the next chapter:

> They marched up over the broad plain of the earth and surrounded the camp of the saints and the beloved city, but fire came down from heaven and consumed them, and the devil who had deceived them was thrown into the lake of fire and sulfur where the beast and the false prophet were, and they will be tormented day and night forever and ever. (Revelation 20:9–10)

## The Thousand Years

In Revelation 20, John saw another angel coming down from heaven to bind Satan, throw him in the pit, and seal it for a thousand years. This scene comes after the defeat of the beast and false prophet in Revelation 19, so traditional Bible scholars have assumed the thousand years of Satan's captivity will come after Jesus returns and establishes His kingdom on Earth.

But Revelation 20 presents the thousand years of Satan's captivity before the final battle where Satan is defeated. The confusion comes because scenes are presented in Revelation from both sides of the scroll: we have the perspective from heaven and the perspective from Earth. John saw the final battle from two perspectives in scenes from Revelation 19 and 20. We see this kind of repetition many times in Revelation because the scenes jump back and forth between the messages on both sides of the two-sided scroll.

The thousand years of Satan's captivity began when Jesus was raised from the dead. Jesus's victory over Satan occurred over two thousand years ago at His resurrection, not in the future as most Bible scholars insist. This was the first resurrection: when Jesus was resurrected, He defeated sin and death, and He bruised Satan's head (Genesis 3:15). This is the mortal wound on the head of the beast in Revelation 13:3. The wound appeared to be healed after Satan was released from his prison and began to deceive the world.

Followers of Jesus who were killed for their faith were also resurrected and reigned with Jesus:

> Also I saw the souls of those who had been beheaded for the testimony of Jesus and for the word of God, and those who had not worshiped the beast or its image and had not received its mark on their foreheads or their hands. They came to life and reigned with Christ for a thousand years. (Revelation 20:4)

When Jesus was dying on the cross, He said, *"It is finished."* When He died, the curtain in the temple was ripped, the Spirit of God left the temple to live among His people, the sun was darkened, and there was a great earthquake. Followers of Jesus rose from the dead and walked around the city.[1]

When Jesus ascended to heaven after His resurrection, He sat on the throne of God and began His reign in heaven. He was given complete authority over heaven and Earth:

> Jesus came and said to them, "All authority in heaven and on earth has been given to me." (Matthew 28:18)

Jesus was given all authority over Earth but He does not yet reign. Sin and evil still prevail. The followers of Jesus are fighting the battle between good and evil, continuing to endure tremendous suffering and physical death. At some point after Jesus's resurrection, perhaps around 1000 AD, Satan was released from his prison. He is now the prince of this world and has been busy deceiving people for centuries:

> Then I saw an angel coming down from heaven, holding in his hand the key to the bottomless pit and a great chain. And he seized the dragon, that ancient serpent, who is the devil and Satan, and bound him for a thousand years, and threw him into the pit, and shut it and sealed it over him, so that he might not deceive the nations any longer, until

> the thousand years were ended. After that he must be released for a little while. (Revelation 20:1–3)

After the resurrection and ascension of Jesus, Satan was locked up for a thousand years to give the Church an opportunity to grow and develop. During the first millennial, Christianity became the world's largest religion. But Satan was released in about 1000 AD. He has since been deceiving the world and even parts of the Church. The Christian Church has been divided and deceived. Many churches have strayed from the truth presented in the Bible —much like some of the churches in the first few chapters of Revelation did. I believe the false prophet in Revelation represents those in the Christian church who have abandoned biblical teaching.

Christianity is now in decline and rivaled by Islam. Christians and Jews are under attack around the world and increasingly in America. Federal and state governments in America are attempting to force Christians to support and even participate in godlessness: Christian doctors, for instance, are forced to perform abortions; pastors and businesses are forced to participate in same-sex marriages (i.e. pastors officiating weddings or bakers forced to bake a wedding cake); employees of certain corporations are forced to celebrate PRIDE month; and Christian parents are forced to allow their children to have sex-change surgery.

America's enemies are working together to bring about our downfall, and American politicians are destroying our country from within through reckless deficit spending, energy regulations, the weakening of our military, and the promotion of sexual immorality and racial division. Even as President Trump attempts to reverse these absurdities, powerful forces are working against him and America. The courts, the media, and progressive Democrats are fighting against everything he is trying to do. Satan's mass deceptions continue around the world. It appears we are near the time described in Revelation when God's wrath is poured onto the earth, Babylon is destroyed, and Jesus returns.

## The Destruction of Babylon the Great: The United States of America

One of the angels who pours a bowl of God's wrath onto the earth also showed John the destruction of the *great city* that will occur during this period of horrific plagues (Revelation 17 and 18). This *great city* is likely the United States of America.

> Come, I will show you the judgment of
> the great prostitute who is seated on many
> waters, with whom the kings of the earth have

> committed sexual immorality, and with the wine of whose sexual immorality the dwellers on earth have become drunk. (Revelation 17:1–2)

If you doubt our once-Christian nation could be called a prostitute by God, consider the facts—and remember God also called Israel a prostitute before He destroyed it (see Ezekiel 16). The wealth of the US has created rich corporate and political tyrants all around the world. The US is the largest producer and exporter of pornography, sex trafficking, homosexuality, same-sex marriage, and transgenderism. We are the world's largest consumer of illegal drugs and sex slavery. And we are doing more to dismantle Judeo-Christian values in the world than any other nation.

In Revelation 17, the prostitute—who represents America —is riding the beast which represents the nations that comprise the world's political and economic system. It is easy to see how this description applies to America today. As the world's military superpower, the most powerful economic system, and the dominant cultural influencer, America *rides* all the nations of the world. But the world hates the dominance of America and is plotting to destroy us. The *ten horns* on the beast represent the ten nations that will lead the effort to destroy the US:

> The ten horns that you saw, they and the beast will hate the prostitute. They will make her desolate and naked, and devour her flesh and burn her up with fire. (Revelation 17:16)

As the cataclysmic events of the end times approach, Christians should expect the apostate church—the second beast—to empower the secular progressive/socialist/communist world system and force believers to follow the first beast, the one-world political system:

> It exercises all the authority of the first beast in its presence, and makes the earth and its inhabitants worship the first beast. (Revelation 13:12)

We are approaching the time described in Revelation 17 when Satan becomes a man and is appointed the leader of the world system. The nations of the world will give him all their authority with the goal of destroying the United States and Israel.

The beast and the nations of the world are already plotting to destroy the United States and Israel. China, Russia, Iran, and other nations are working together to undermine our currency and destroy our economic system with scams of climate change, racism, and LGBTQ sexual perversion. These scam campaigns are largely funded by foreign governments:

> China voluntarily provided and mobilized $45 billion to support efforts to curb emissions or adapt to climate impacts in developing countries (or $4.5 billion a year, on average), amounting to roughly 6% of the total climate finance from developed countries during the same 10-year period.[2]

These spending levels understate the amount of money China is spending to undermine America with scams. Much of their money is given as underreported grants to universities that are more than happy to promote a radical progressive agenda:

> The PRC (People's Republic of China) is the largest source of foreign donations to US universities since 2013. The tuition paid by Chinese students is worth an estimated $12 billion per year. Chinese sources have participated in donations or contracts worth more than $426 million to US universities since 2011.[3]

Don't be deceived. China has no interest in reducing $CO_2$ emissions. Over the last several years, China has opened more than one new coal-powered electric generating plant a week.[4] But China knows that eliminating fossil fuels for the rest of the world will weaken and eventually destroy the United States and our Western allies.

The great prostitute in Revelation 17 is called Babylon. The original Babylon does not exist today; it was destroyed before the birth of Jesus. Only one nation in the world now fits the description of Babylon given in Revelation, and it is the United States of America:

> She has become a dwelling place for
> demons . . .
> For all nations have drunk
> the wine of the passion of her sexual
> immorality . . .
> and the merchants of the earth have grown
> rich from the power of her luxuri*ous living*.
> (Revelation 18:2–3)

Babylon was a major city and a great empire. I suspect the Babylon in Revelation represents both a large port city and a nation. The description in Revelation suggests the burning city may be New York and the nation, the United States. New York has been targeted by American enemies for decades because it represents America's economic power. It's home to both the second largest port in the US and the New York Stock Exchange, the largest stock exchange in the world.

As New York and the United States are being destroyed, God will rapture His people from around the world. All God's people will be removed from Earth:

> Then I heard another voice from heaven
> saying,
> "Come out of her, my people,
> lest you take part in her sins,
> lest you share in her plagues;
> for her sins are heaped high as heaven,
> and God has remembered her iniquities."
> (Revelation 18:4)

Revelation foretells the destruction of a large port city—perhaps New York—by fire. This suggests a nuclear attack that would throw the whole American economic system into chaos. Revelation describes the scene of cargo ships anchored offshore watching in horror from a distance:

> All shipmasters and seafaring men, sailors and all whose trade is on the sea, stood far off and cried out as they saw the smoke of her burning (Revelation 18:17–18)

The following table presents the perspective from both sides of the scroll of God's wrath poured out on Earth and the rapture of God's people from Babylon and *across the earth* (Revelation 14:16).

| God's Wrath and the Harvest of the Earth | | |
|---|---|---|
| ***Perspective from Heaven*** *(first side of the scroll)* | ***Meaning*** | ***Perspective from Earth*** *(second side of the scroll)* |
| *So he who sat on the cloud swung his sickle across the earth, and the earth was reaped.* (Revelation 14:16) | God's people in America and from around the world are taken to heaven. | Believers are raptured from Babylon.<br><br>*Come out of her, my people, lest you take part in her sins, lest you share in her plagues.* (Revelation 18:4) |
| The end of time begins with the pouring out from heaven seven bowls of God's wrath. | Those who are left on Earth will experience unimaginable horrors. | *So the first angel went and poured out his bowl on the earth, and harmful and painful sores came upon the people who bore the mark of the beast and worshiped its image.* (Revelation 16:2) |

| God's Wrath and the Harvest of the Earth | |
|---|---|
| ***Perspective from Heaven*** *(first side of the scroll)* | ***Perspective from Earth*** *(second side of the scroll)* |
| *Then I heard a loud voice from the temple telling the seven angels, "Go and pour out on the earth the seven bowls of the wrath of God."* (Revelation 16:1) | *The second angel poured out his bowl into the sea, and it became like the blood of a corpse, and every living thing died that was in the sea.* (Revelation 16:3)<br><br>*The third angel poured out his bowl into the rivers and the springs of water, and they became blood.* (Revelation 16:4)<br><br>*The fourth angel poured out his bowl on the sun, and it was allowed to scorch people with fire.* (Revelation 16:8)<br><br>*The fifth angel poured out his bowl on the throne of the beast, and its kingdom was plunged into darkness.* (Revelation 16:10)<br><br>*The sixth angel poured out his bowl on the great river Euphrates, and its water was dried up, to prepare the way for the kings from the east.* (Revelation 16:12) |

| God's Wrath and the Harvest of the Earth | |
|---|---|
| ***Perspective from Heaven*** *(first side of the scroll)* | ***Perspective from Earth*** *(second side of the scroll)* |
| *Then I heard a loud voice from the temple telling the seven angels, "Go and pour out on the earth the seven bowls of the wrath of God."* (Revelation 16:1) | *The seventh angel poured out his bowl into the air, and a loud voice came out of the temple, from the throne, saying, "It is done!" And there were flashes of lightning, rumblings, peals of thunder, and a great earthquake such as there had never been since man was on the earth, so great was that earthquake. The great city was split into three parts, and the cities of the nations fell, and God remembered Babylon the great, to make her drain the cup of the wine of the fury of his wrath. And every island fled away, and no mountains were to be found. And great hailstones, about one hundred pounds each, fell from heaven on people; and they cursed God for the plague of the hail, because the plague was so severe.* (Revelation 16:17–21) |

## Warnings to All People on Earth

In Revelation 14, three angels proclaim the gospel of Jesus to all who live on Earth. This happens after the destruction of Babylon (the United States?) and probably after the rapture of God's people. It appears to be a warning and the last-chance call to repentance to all who are left on Earth. Many of God's people who have not accepted Jesus will be left behind after the rapture. They will experience the horrors of the last days.

> Then I saw another angel flying directly overhead, with an eternal gospel to proclaim to those who dwell on earth, to every nation and tribe and language and people. (Revelation 14:6)

The angels give three pronouncements and warnings to the people left on Earth:

> "Fear God and give him glory, because the hour of his judgment has come, and worship him who made heaven and earth, the sea and the springs of water."
>
> Another angel, a second, followed, saying, "Fallen, fallen is Babylon the great, she who made all nations drink the wine of the passion of her sexual immorality."
>
> And another angel, a third, followed them, saying with a loud voice, "If anyone worships the beast and its image and receives a mark on his forehead or on his hand, he also will drink the wine of God's wrath, poured full strength into the cup of his anger, and he will be tormented with fire and sulfur in the presence

> of the holy angels and in the presence of the Lamb." (Revelation 14:7–10)

## The Mark of the Beast

The mark of the beast is mentioned several times in Revelation, and the third angel warns of the consequences to be faced by any who receive the mark on their forehead or hand.

The mark of the beast is described as the number 666. We are told in Revelation 13 the second beast—the false prophet—*causes* everyone to accept the mark of the first beast. This should alarm all believers because the false prophet is the apostate Church:

> Also it causes all, both small and great, both rich and poor, both free and slave, to be marked on the right hand or the forehead, so that no one can buy or sell unless he has the mark, that is, the name of the beast or the number of its name. This calls for wisdom: let the one who has understanding calculate the number of the beast, for it is the number of a man, and his number is 666. (Revelation 13:16–18)

I believe the number 666 represents the secular world system, known in our time as socialism, communism, and, now in America, the progressive Democrat party. I don't think it will be an actual mark on foreheads and hands. Perhaps it's a reference to the Old Testament Jewish custom of men wearing on their foreheads a headband with a little box that contained Scripture verses and reminders of God's goodness. This "mark" on the forehead reminded Jews what they believed.

In Revelation, the mark on foreheads likely represents what people believe. The mark on hands is what they do—their works. The warnings in Revelation are for people not to accept the beliefs or the lifestyles of the sinful world around us. Believers are called to be separate.

The symbolic mark of the beast has been around since the beginning of time. It is the mark of mankind. Only the blood of Jesus can remove that mark. However, as we approach the last days, it is possible people may be forced to accept an actual physical chip implanted in their hands or forehead if they want to buy or sell anything. We already see evidence of this with banks choosing to freeze customers' accounts for political reasons. This will get much worse soon. Most of our money, investments, and savings are already digital, and it will be easy for political leaders to freeze our assets, control what we can buy, or even take everything we own without notice.

## The Stage Is Set for the Final Battle and the Return of Christ

Revelation 20:7–10 summarizes the events that happened after Satan was released in about 1000 AD: he deceives the nations of the world, he organizes them for battle, he leads the nations to surround and attack Jerusalem, he and all the nations are defeated, he is thrown into the *lake of fire* with the beast and the false prophet, and they will all be tormented forever:

> When the thousand years are ended, Satan will be released from his prison and will come out to deceive the nations that are at the four corners of the earth, Gog and Magog, to gather them for battle; their number is like the sand of the sea. And they marched up over the broad plain of the earth and surrounded the camp of the saints and the beloved city, but fire came down from heaven and consumed them, and the devil who had deceived them was thrown into the lake of fire and sulfur where the beast and the false prophet were, and they will be tormented day and night forever and ever. (Revelation 20:7–10)

## The Great Judgment

After the defeat of Satan and the world system, the physical world disappears. All the people who have lived on Earth since Adam appear before God to be judged. These people are separated into two groups: God's people whose names are written in the book of life and all the others. Everyone—except God's people whose sin was paid for and removed by the blood of Jesus—will be judged according to their actions and sin. Everyone whose name is not written in the book of life will be thrown into the lake of fire (hell) for eternity:

> Then I saw a great white throne and him who was seated on it. From his presence earth and sky fled away, and no place was found for them. And I saw the dead, great and small, standing before the throne, and books were opened. Then another book was opened, which is the book of life. And the dead were judged by what was written in the books, according to what they had done. And the sea gave up the dead who were in it, Death and Hades gave up the dead who were in them, and they were judged, each one of them, according to what they had done. Then Death and Hades were thrown into the lake of fire.

> This is the second death, the lake of fire. And if anyone's name was not found written in the book of life, he was thrown into the lake of fire." (Revelation 20:11–15)

## A New Heaven on a New Earth

The last two chapters of Revelation contain the most exciting news in the entire Bible for God's people. God completes His plan to unite the physical and the spiritual worlds and creates a new heaven on a new Earth. God will live with His people on a new and perfected Earth. There will be no more pain, suffering, or death:

> I heard a loud voice from the throne saying, "Behold, the dwelling place of God is with man. He will dwell with them, and they will be his people, and God himself will be with them as their God. He will wipe away every tear from their eyes, and death shall be no more, neither shall there be mourning, nor crying, nor pain anymore, for the former things have passed away. (Revelation 21:3–4)

## What Believers Should Expect from 2025 Until Jesus Returns

The most important action for you—and every person on Earth—is to confirm that your name is written in the book of life. Repent, relent, and give your life to Jesus. If you can hear Him call, if you can sense Him knocking at the door of your heart, you know you are His, and you must respond.

Believers can expect to see more persecution of Christians and Jews. We will also see biblical values and truths diminished and even eliminated from public life. Political leaders like President Trump can only delay the inevitable. There will be great deceptions and increasing pressure on Christians to accept the lies and lifestyles of godless people. Many Christian leaders will begin to support and promote anti-biblical worldviews and pressure believers to display a mark to show their allegiance to the world. It will become increasingly difficult for biblical Christians and Jews to get jobs and to buy things they need.

Conflicts will increase around the world, and violent divisions will break out among Americans. A massive financial crisis will occur in America, and the dollar will lose its value due to the massive debt of the federal government. We should all pray and hope President Trump and future leaders will reverse America's decline and delay our destruction. If Americans repent, God can change anything!

China, Russia, Iran, and many European nations will conspire to destroy the Unites States because of its protection of Israel and its economic and military dominance. President Trump's confrontations with countries taking advantage of America has already encouraged the nations of the world to organize against the United States. A great and charismatic world leader will soon emerge who is the incarnation of Satan. Most of the nations of the world will give their allegiance to this leader.

As America and other nations devolve into financial and cultural chaos, God will rapture His people from all around the world. With Christians gone from the world, Satan will lead the nations to attack America with nuclear weapons. New York will likely be the first city attacked. America will be helpless to respond.

God will pour out His wrath on the world as Satan and his coalition of nations surround Israel for the final attack. As they approach Jerusalem, God will strike them all with fire from heaven, and the world will end. Then all of God's people will return to a new heaven on a new Earth and live forever in the presence of Jesus.

## *Chapter 8*

# Politics, Progressivism, and Biblical Truth

"IF YOU WANT to keep your friends," I've been told, "don't talk about politics and religion." It's good advice, but these are two of the most important subjects in our lives. Politics is the continuous process of negotiating how we live together in our families, our churches, our communities; how we relate to our friends; and how we are governed. Religion determines what we believe about God, how we view the world, and how we behave.

Politics in the private sector is usually informal and voluntary, but the politics of government is a more formal process producing laws and requirements that control our lives. Government can either guarantee our freedoms or restrict them.

Religion in America is voluntary although during America's first two centuries, religion was often imposed by cultural norms and public shaming. Today, public shaming is more likely directed at those who take religion seriously. Why the change? And why do I feel compelled to combine an unorthodox view of the Bible with a seemingly partisan analysis of politics?

What may appear an attempt to shoehorn a round peg into a square hole is, I believe, the only perspective from which we can understand the American condition. Biblical Christianity is the antidote for an oppressive secular government. But as the credibility of biblical truth has declined, our government has grown increasingly large, oppressive—and progressive.

## America Is Great because America Is Good

Alexis de Tocqueville, a French historian who studied early America after its founding, is often credited with the observation "America is great because she is good, and if America ever ceases to be good, she will cease to be great."

This quote has been used by Christians to highlight America's religious founding, but it cannot be found in any of de Tocqueville's writings. Progressives in America have criticized people of faith who have used the quote to buttress their belief that Christian virtues made America a great nation. While the quote above may not be an exact quote from de Tocqueville, the following is:

> Despotism may govern without faith, but liberty cannot. Religion is much more necessary in the republic which they [Americans] set forth in glowing colors than in the monarchy which they attack; and it is more needed in democratic republics than in any others. How is it possible that society should escape destruction if the moral tie be not strengthened in proportion as the political tie is relaxed? and what can be done with a people which is its own master, if it be not submissive to the Divinity?[1]

Alexis de Tocqueville clearly understood that people will either be mastered by God or government. The prevalence of biblical religious faith supplants the need for excessive government, and the absence of true religion is an invitation to government tyranny.

## There Is Still Much Good in America

My criticism of America's loss of religious faith and morality should not be mistaken for loss of love for my country. I have spent much of my life fighting in the private and political spheres for America and our people. The ideals and history of America have produced much more virtue than vice. But the foundation for virtue in

America is being replaced by sinister forces creating a biblical Babylon.

I lived most of my life insulated from the evil now enveloping our country. My family, neighbors, church, business associates, and community were mostly people of faith, political conservatives, and virtuous citizens. During my first forty-seven years growing up, raising a family, and working in the business world, I was naïve and blind to the darkness that was replacing the light all around America. My children went to a Christian school where they were taught principles for good citizenship and success in life. The goodness in my small sphere made me very optimistic about the future of our country.

My experience in politics in Washington, DC, and my travels around the world have, however, shocked my reality and shaken my hope for America's future. The 2024 election with the re-election of President Trump and Republican majorities renewed my optimism but I am incredulous that half of the country voted for candidates and ideals fundamentally opposed to common sense and biblical principles.

I am painfully aware of the shortcomings of Republicans. In fact, I spent much of my time in the U.S. House and the Senate criticizing Republicans and trying to un-elect some of my Republican colleagues. Many of them had no intention of keeping the promises they made during their campaigns. And most of the Republican leadership in Washington over the past two decades adopted many progressive ideas, especially their positions on globalism, military interventions, and trade. Republicans are all sinners and often fall short of reasonable expectations.

I also developed friendships with colleagues in the House and Senate who were Democrats. When I first came to Congress in 1998, I attended fellowships and Bible studies where I prayed with Democrats. We even agreed on basic political principles and goals even though we argued about the proper role of government. But I no longer have any common ground with Democrats in Washington. The reasonable Democrats have been rooted out and replaced by radical progressives who have no resemblance to traditional Democrats.

## The Good News and the Bad News of the 2024 Election

In 2024, Donald Trump was re-elected president by winning both the popular vote and the electoral college. The odds were stacked against him. He was vilified in the media, indicted and convicted by federal and state Democrat prosecutors, and massively outspent. Yet, somehow, Trump won in an electoral landslide. The majority of voters liked what Trump was selling and they weren't buying the messages from the Democrats.

Despite Trump's decisive victory, it is important to remember that nearly half of Americans voted for Kamala Harris and progressive Democrats. Did they know what they were voting for?

The Democrats spent billions of dollars telling Americans that Trump and his Republican party were racists, bigots, white supremacists, misogynists, homophobes, Nazis, and other personal slurs. They offered very little criticism of Republican policies except for provably false accusations such as Republicans will cut Social Security and Medicare and cater to the rich. (The rich give exponentially more money to the Democrats: the rich know who their friends are.)

The top-priority policy for Democrats in the 2024 presidential election was to force states to allow abortion until the day of birth under the banner of reproductive rights for women. Think I'm exaggerating? In 2024, every Democrat in the Senate (except now-independent Joe Manchin) voted for a national law requiring all states to allow abortion until the day of birth. A Google search will only give you articles claiming this is "mostly false," but the fact is, the bill all Democrats supported had no restrictions on abortion.

Apparently, almost half of American voters believed the slurs against Republicans and voted for the Democrat Party in 2024. Whether they knew it or not, their votes supported the following progressive policies:

- Men in women's sports
- Transgender surgeries for children
- Transgender surgery for prisoners paid for by taxpayers
- Forced celebration of homosexuality (PRIDE Month)
- Forcing pastors and businesses to participate and /or support same-sex marriages
- Abortion until the day of birth
- Forcing Christian doctors and hospitals to perform abortions
- Open borders
- Climate change being the world's most serious threat
- Eliminating gasoline engines in cars
- Replacing natural gas and nuclear electricity generation with wind and solar
- No voter identification requirements
- Allowing noncitizens and prisoners to vote
- Equity: government-mandated equality of outcomes
- Hiring based on race and sexual preferences (DEI)

- No school choice
- Government healthcare for everyone (Medicare for all)
- No balanced budget requirement for Congress
- Teaching critical race theory (CRT) and the premise that America was founded on racism
- No biblical teachings in schools or application of biblical principles in government agencies
- Forcing churches and Christian organizations to hire non-Christian employees (Equal Rights Amendment).

Traditional Democrats will deny they support many of these policies, but everyone who votes for Democrats is advancing all of them. The Democrat Party is now controlled by radical progressives. It is inconceivable to me that any informed and thoughtful Christian could vote for a progressive Democrat.

## The Declining Relevance of the Christian Church

Why do nearly half of Americans support these radical progressive policies? They don't. Surveys show approximately 70 percent of Americans oppose most of the policy positions listed above. Many of these voters still support Democrats because they either don't know the Democrat Party is the primary sponsor of progressive initiatives or because they believe the slurs against Republicans. This ignorance is the result of media coverups and Republican stupidity.

Republicans often blame radical progressive ideas on the left. Many Americans don't know what the left means or don't associate the left with the Democrat Party. Every time Republicans blame bad policy of the left, they give Democrats a free pass. If Americans ever discover the truth, the Democrat Party will likely fade into obscurity.

Christian pastors and leaders should tell Americans the truth, and all of us Christians must defend biblical truth and tell the truth about political parties and policy positions. Pastors must be shepherds and watchmen who protect and warn their congregations. We often hear the excuse churches should avoid politics, but this is nonsense. Most of the issues listed above are biblical issues, and the Church should be leading the fight against them. Christian stewardship requires God's people to fulfill their responsibilities as citizens (see, for instance, Romans 13:1–7).

If Christians don't fill America with righteousness, our nation will be filled with evil. We cannot allow what is good to be called evil, and we cannot allow what is evil to be called good.

Unfortunately, the relevance of both biblical truth and the Christian church has declined significantly in

America. The face of Moses may be carved in stone in the House of Representatives, but the laws God gave to Moses are now anathema to most Democrat lawmakers.

## The Rise of Progressivism in America

What is progressivism? It means leaving the past behind and progressing to the future. It means forgetting our history, throwing off traditions and religious restraints, and moving boldly into uncharted waters. Conservatives have a very different approach: they identify the principles and values that have worked in the past and apply them to the challenges of the future.

In practice, we have seen progressive Democrats distort and vilify America's history, tear down historic statues, denigrate America's founders, criticize free market capitalism, promote equity instead of merit, and sponsor massive deceptions such as climate change, COVID hysteria, systemic racism, and the nobility of sexual immorality.

Progressives often use words like *modernization* and phrases such as presidential candidate Kamala Harris's *unburdened by the past*. They obsess with eliminating personal pronouns indicating "gender" and have introduced legislation to eliminate *husband* and *wife* from government documents. Concepts such as the traditional family, hard work, and personal responsibility have been labeled vestiges of white supremacy.

For students of world history, the ideology and language of progressives should be very familiar. It is a replica of communism! The following description of communism should be profoundly foreboding to anyone familiar with today's Democrat Party:

> It uses the slogans of "democracy," "equality," and "social justice" to infiltrate the fields of education, media, art, and law, bringing people under its banner without their awareness. At yet other times, it calls itself "socialism," "progressivism," "liberalism," "neo-Marxism," and other leftist terms. Sometimes it holds up seemingly righteous banners such as pacifism, environmentalism, globalism, and political correctness. Other times, it supports vanguard art, sexual liberation, legalization of drugs, homosexuality, and other indulgencies in human desires, giving the mistaken impression that it's part of a popular trend.[2]

It is an illusion to believe that allowing people to vote for their leaders will protect them from the progressive shroud of communism. Ryszard Legutko, a Polish professor, member of the European Parliament, and author of *The Demon in Democracy*, reveals how the new liberal democracies in eastern Europe quickly and subtly adopted the tenets of communism after they were supposedly liberated from communism. They failed to see how communism was perverting their democracies:

> Both communism and liberal democracy are regimes whose intent is to change reality for the better. They are—to use the jargon—modernization projects. Both are nourished by the belief that the world cannot be tolerated as it is and that it should be changed: that the old should be replaced with the new. Both systems strongly and—so to speak—impatiently intrude into the social fabric and both justify their intrusion with the argument that it leads to the improvement of the state of affairs by "modernizing" it."[3]

In America, the word *liberal* has become a negative, so the radical wing of the Democrat Party has adopted *progressive* to describe how they are moving away from the traditions of the past. They have also begun to emphasize the word *democracy* to brainwash Americans to believe America was founded to be a national democracy where the majority rules instead of the constitutional state-based representative republic that the Founders actually designed.

Like citizens in the liberal democracies of eastern Europe, most progressive Democrats in America don't know they are promoting a communist agenda. It would be difficult to find a progressive Democrat who openly supports communism. Few even know the progressive agenda mirrors communist ideas. Their bent toward communist ideology is not a well-planned conspiracy. It is the natural result of a godless void in the human heart and in the culture at large. If a glass of water is poured out, it is immediately filled with air. The same is true with our culture. When Judeo-Christian biblical values are removed, America is immediately filled with godless progressive values. No conspiracy is needed.

When the nation of Israel escaped Egypt and finally took possession of the Promised Land, God wanted them to live in freedom with Him as their king. He gave them priests to keep their focus on God's laws and judges to ensure justice. But the Jewish people wanted a human king like other nations had. God warned them against submitting to earthly power but they insisted. When God gave them a human king, Israel adopted the ways of other nations, a path that eventually led to their destruction. This has been the course of mankind.

Throughout recorded history, civilizations have been controlled by small groups of elites—kings, dictators, feudal lords, and emperors. The masses lived as peasants and subsistence farmers. The advent of

Jesus Christ and the Bible changed the world order. Judeo-Christian values became the foundation of western civilization. Individual freedom and personal responsibility created the most advanced cultures in the world. Entrepreneurship and free market capitalism lifted millions out of poverty. Biblical values led to the abolition of slavery, equal rights for women, and compassion for the poor and disabled.

America was founded on the belief all people have God-given inalienable rights such as life, liberty, and the pursuit of happiness. Government did not bequeath rights to American citizens. The government of the United States was established to protect the God-ordained rights of every citizen.

Progressive Democrats have a very different view of the role of government. They believe, as do communists, the federal government should control and manage the lives of Americans. But it is not possible for government to control a people who believe God is in control and holds eternity in His hands. That's why progressives seek to diminish and discredit the Bible. Without the Bible as a source of unchangeable truth, progressives have re-created God into a benevolent sanction for their anti-biblical policies.

Progressives glorify premarital sex, homosexuality, same-sex marriage, transgender surgeries on children, and pornography. If these practices are right, the Bible is wrong. Progressives block school choice so Christian parents are forced to send their children to godless schools where they are taught the universe was created by accident and life randomly evolved. If children believe this account of creation, they don't believe the Bible. Some progressives may feign religious faith, but their religion is man-made and has little resemblance to true biblical faith.

It is important for me to clarify my comments about sexual immorality. I am not suggesting Americans should not have the right to live as they choose. There should be no legal prohibition against premarital sex or homosexuality. But the killing of unborn children and sex-change surgeries for children are very different issues, and the government should prohibit these practices. Christians should love everyone as fellow sinners.

However, neither the government nor any other organization should have the power to force anyone to accept or practice behavior they believe is wrong. Christians should have the right to practice their biblical morality in their lives and freely express their views—and non-Christians should have that same freedom. Christian parents should not be forced to send their children to schools that teach an antibiblical worldview. The money the government spends on public education should follow students to the schools of their parents' choice.

Progressive Democrats and their media allies should not be the arbiters of what is right and wrong, and Christians should not be allowed to impose their beliefs on non-Christians. All Americans should respect the rights of everyone to decide what they believe and how they should live within the bounds of law.

## The Negative Impact of Progressivism on America

### *Promoting Fatherless Homes, Poverty, and Crime*

Progressive Democrat policies have weakened the American family, the foundation of tradition and societal health. Democrats' welfare policies discourage marriage and work. But for decades, Democrats refused to work with Republicans to revise policies that are obviously detrimental to the people they are supposed to help. Why? Because the Democrat Party thrives on government dependency. A dependent voter is a dependable vote for Democrats.

The consequences of progressive welfare policies have devastated several generations of Americans. The following is a summary of some of the social pathologies caused by the welfare policies of progressive Democrats.

### *Single-Parent Households*

The United States has the *highest rate* of children in single-parent households of any nation in the world.

- There are over 18 million fatherless children in the US.
- Fathers are absent from approximately 80% of single-parent homes.
- Fatherless families are 4x more likely to live in poverty than . . . married-couple families.
- Fatherless children are more likely to abuse drugs and show signs of delinquent behavior.
- Children from single-parent families are twice as likely to suffer from mental health problems as those living with married parents.
- Data suggests 84% of homeless families are headed by women, and 90% of homeless and runaway children come from fatherless homes.
- 63% of youth suicides are from fatherless homes.
- 85% of children who exhibit behavior disorders are from fatherless homes.
- 70% of juveniles in state-operated institutions come from single-parent homes.
- Most adolescents who enter the justice system have suffered from parental abandonment, substance abuse, or a dysfunctional household. In

a study of 75 juvenile delinquents, 66% experienced fatherlessness, 20% had never lived with their father, and 25% had an alcoholic father.

- In a study of 56 school shootings, only 10 of the shooters (18%) were raised in a stable home with both biological parents. 82% grew up in either an unstable family environment or grew up without both biological parents together.
- Children living absent their biological father are 2 to 3 times more likely to be expelled or suspended at some time.
- Girls who feel closeness to their father are 75% less likely to have a teen birth. One study showed girls whose father left the home before they were 5 years old were 8 times more likely to become pregnant as adolescents.
- Children who feel closeness to their father are 80% less likely to spend time in jail.
- When children have an actively involved father, they are 33% less likely to drop out of school and 43% more likely to get A's.
- Children in single-parent homes are more likely to have low self-esteem, depression, anxiety, and more suicidal thoughts and attempts.[4]

Progressive Democrats blame the high rate of imprisonment of Black Americans on racism. But policies encouraging fatherless homes are the real cause. Nearly 70 percent of black children are born to unmarried mothers.[5] But Democrats won't address the real cause of suffering among Black Americans because racism is their most powerful political strategy.

Federal welfare policies create more poverty and, consequently, the need for more welfare spending. The US spent "$1.048 trillion in fiscal year 2024, or 16% of all federal outlays."[6] None of these programs are designed to help the poor become more independent.

### *Sexual Promiscuity and Perversion*

The elimination of biblical morality has a high social cost. According to the Centers for Disease Control, over half of Americans will contract a sexually transmitted disease during their lifetime. STDs can cause serious health issues, loss of productivity, and even death. The US spends nearly $20 billion every year to treat STDs with the largest portion of this directed to HIV patients.[7]

### *Pornography*

The use of online pornography has become America's most serious addiction. Approximately 70 percent of men and 40 percent of women view pornography every year. Only 14 percent believe the use of pornography is wrong.[8]

> Pornography can have negative consequences for both the user and his or her intimate partner. Some of the common damaging effects of pornography for users can include addiction, isolation, increased aggression, distorted beliefs and perceptions about relationships and sexuality, negative feelings about themselves, and neglecting other areas of their lives.[9]

Pornography confuses a person's sexual orientation and can lead to homosexual behavior, gender confusion, transgenderism, and the destruction of traditional heterosexual relationships and marriages. Unlike drugs that can be eliminated from our bodies, it is impossible to unsee pornographic images.

Pornography has also become a cancer on the Christian church. Pornography use by Christians is about the same as the general population. Even more concerning, half of Christians believe there is nothing wrong with using pornography. Many pastors now struggle with this addiction. This is perhaps the best example of how the church is being shaped by the culture instead of shaping the culture.

> In the church, pastors are now more likely to report a personal history of porn use (67

> percent versus 57 percent nine years ago). Nearly one in five pastors say they currently struggle with porn. And among Christians who have attended services within the last month, more than half say they view pornography at least occasionally.[10]

Not only do most Americans use pornography, over 60 percent of the porn websites are hosted in the US with the large majority of those located in California.[11] We are literally polluting the world with filth and dragging many young children into the production of porn.

### *America's State and Federal Governments Are Destroying Our Culture*

Government welfare policies have weakened the American family structure. Laws also protect and promote sexual deviance. Laws protect the pornography industry. State-sponsored lotteries are now the largest promoters of gambling addiction (annual costs $14 billion). Online sports gambling has exploded since its legalization. Gambling breaks up families and causes job loss, bankruptcies, and many other problems. Open borders and illegal immigration have flooded America with criminals, drug dealers, sex traffickers, and millions who don't share our values or common heritage.

The list of destructive government policies is extensive. It is difficult to find anything the federal or state governments are doing to encourage wholesome and productive behavior. In a free society, citizens should have the right to adopt destructive behaviors, but it is unacceptable for governments to encourage and even pay for destructive lifestyles that hurt everyone and weaken our country. Even worse, America is using our economic and military prowess to force other countries to adopt our progressive cultural values.

America is now over $37 trillion in debt and essentially bankrupt. We are also morally bankrupt. The world is taking note of both. Even Russia forbids Americans from adopting Russian children because of the risk of homosexual parents and transgender surgeries. Today, 77 percent of American youth don't qualify for military service because of obesity or other physical and mental disqualifiers.[12] Birth rates in America are at historic lows—well below replacement rates. America is clearly on the decline.

It is difficult to be optimistic about America's future. But I believe we who are God's people can turn our country around. We need to stop sitting on the sidelines while claiming everything's in God's hands. It's not. God put it all in our hands. We are His hands, His feet, and His voice—and we must act now!

# Conclusion

"SAY IT ISN'T so!" I suspect most of my readers are completely distracted at this point by the proposition America the beautiful may soon be destroyed because of our evil ways. But perhaps God will grant us a reprieve?

## A Call to National Repentance

In the book of Jonah, Nineveh was an exceedingly large and evil city. God sent Jonah to warn the people in Nineveh that He was going to destroy them and their city in forty days. After a brief detour in the belly of a fish, Jonah went to Nineveh and called on the people to repent. To Jonah's surprise, the people believed God, and their king issued a decree for all the people to repent:

> "Let everyone turn from his evil way and from the violence that is in his hands. Who knows?

> God may turn and relent and turn from his fierce anger, so that we may not perish." (Jonah 3:8–9)

Genuine repentance can change God's plans or at least delay them:

> When God saw what they did, how they turned from their evil way, God relented of the disaster that he had said he would do to them, and he did not do it. (Jonah 3:10)

Nineveh was spared for over 200 years until they forgot about God and returned to their evil ways. The dates of end time prophecies cannot be precisely known, but regardless, God's people should repent and turn to God. I am calling on pastors, Christian leaders, and all God's people to lead a national call to repentance. If God's people repent, the Holy Spirit will revive our faith and perhaps restore our nation.

America's revival must be based on truth, and God has given us His truth in Jesus and in His written Word, the Bible. The challenge facing every believer is to search for, to test, and to know what is true. The spirit of the Antichrist is all around us, and deceptions will increase, even in the Church. Every believer should pray for wisdom and seek the truth.

There are several serious deceptions now coming from within the church:

- The Bible is not completely true.
- Jesus is not God.
- Jesus is not the only way to God and eternal life.
- The Bible does not say premarital sex, homosexuality, same-sex marriage, transgenderism, and other forms a sexual immorality are wrong.
- People with immoral lifestyles can be pastors and church leaders.
- The Church should not be involved with politics unless it is in support of climate change, critical race theory, diversity, or social justice.

The Bible is a supernatural document that tells us how and why God created the physical world. It predicts future events, many of which have already come true. Many of the cities and events described in the Bible have been confirmed to be real by archaeologists and historians. The Bible has proved itself true! Dozens of authors in the Bible over thousands of years wrote a consistent message: God loves His people and will save them for eternity.

The main theme of the Bible is, God will save His people and unify heaven and Earth. He does it by becoming a physical man, sacrificing His own life to pay for our sins, rising from the dead to demonstrate His power over death, sending His Holy Spirit to empower and teach His people on Earth, and, finally, creating a new heaven on a new Earth for His people to live for eternity.

The Bible is the best-selling book of all time, and no other document in history even approaches its credibility and authenticity.

The Bible confirms what hundreds of years of scientific research and study have discovered: God created the universe millions of years ago, civilizations have existed on Earth for hundreds of thousands of years, and catastrophic events have occurred on Earth resulting in ice ages, floods, and the extinction of many species of animals and early humans.

The Bible also confirms what we know from relatively recent history: the whole world changed two thousand years ago after the life, death, and resurrection of Jesus Christ. Calendars were changed to begin at Year 0 when Jesus was born. Kingdoms adopted His teachings as Christianity grew to be the largest religion in the world. And now, for over 1,500 years, the Bible has been the source of Judeo-Christian beliefs and values that have guided the development of Europe, America, and the entire Western world. Until recently, the Bible was considered the only standard of truth for a large part of the world.

But just as we've seen in the past, even the Christian church sometimes becomes the enemy of truth. Galileo, a devoted Christian and scientist, was excommunicated by the Catholic Church in 1615 for supporting the theory that the Earth revolves around the sun. Martin Luther, a Catholic monk, was excommunicated by the Catholic Church for espousing obvious biblical truths such as people are saved by faith in Jesus, not by works. Unfortunately, history is replete with Christian martyrs who spoke unwelcome truth and found themselves on the wrong side of a firepit.

Today, the organized church is largely silent on the teachings of evolution in our schools, the celebration of homosexuality and same-sex marriage, the transgender and sex-change craze, critical race theory, social justice nonsense, welfare payments for people who won't work, and many other public policies fundamentally opposed to Judeo-Christian values and principles. These are not only political issues; they are biblical issues in need of Christian input and leadership.

We need Christians to defend the truth of the Bible. In times of great deception, it is *the* only Truth we need. The Bible should never be changed with the times, but the times will illuminate what God wants us to know and what He wants us to do.

God fully expects His revelation to become clearer as we approach the end of time. Events in the world, as well as technology unimaginable when the Bible was written, will bring new insights and meaning to biblical words and passages read by believers for centuries. We should never change any word of Scripture, but we should not be afraid to consider new interpretations of Scripture or to propose new theories about what the Bible really means.

I have concluded that God created the physical world to separate good from evil and to serve as a bridge for His people to cross into the new heaven on a new Earth. God's people are sent to Earth to fight the battle between good and evil. When we obey God's Word and worship Him, we defeat Satan and justify God's mercy on His people.

God is sovereign over all things, but by His own choice He does not yet exert full control over the physical world. He delegates the fight against evil and the advancement of righteousness to His people. We are in a battle against Satan and his demons, and we will all suffer and die in this physical world. The battle between good and evil will be decided by the faithfulness of God's people on Earth. Thankfully, we already know the outcome: God's people win!

God's spiritual family has been passing through the physical world for hundreds of thousands of years. When His creatures die on Earth, their spirits wait under the altar of God until all have passed through.

When all of God's creatures have traveled through the physical world, the current heaven and Earth will disappear. A new heaven on a new Earth will be created for all of God's people to live eternally.

If we seek truth, we will find it. And we can know for certain that the Word of God is truth, and this truth is Jesus—*the way, and the truth, and the life* (John 14:6) His Holy Spirit will lead us to all truth if we seek Him. I'm not asking you to take my word for it. I'm saying, "Seek and you will find."

# Endnotes

### *Preface*

1. greenclimate.fund

2. James T. Areddy, "Research for Sale: How Chinese Money Flows to American Universities," National Association of Independent Colleges and Universities, April 15, 2024, https://www.naicu.edu/news-events/headline-news/2024/04/research-for-sale-how-chinese-money-flows-to-american-universities/

3. The Editorial Team of the *Nine Commentaries on the Communist Party*, *How the Specter of Communism Is Ruling Our World*, *The Epoch Times*, 3//8/2019; updated 5/2/25, 38-39. https://www.theepochtimes.com/article/how-the-specter-of-communism-is-ruling-our-world-list-of-chapters-2658181

### *Introduction*

1. Brian Freeman, "Gallup Poll: Belief in Creationism at All-Time Low," *Newsmax,* July 22, 2024, https://www.newsmax.com/newsfront/gallup-creationism-evolution/2024/07/22/id/1173547/

2. Megan Basham, *Shepherds for Sale: How Evangelical Leaders Traded the Truth for a Leftist Agenda* (Broadside e-books, July 30, 2024).

3. Ronald L. Numbers, *Galileo Goes to Jail and Other Myths about Science and Religion* (Cambridge, MA: Harvard University Press, (8 November 2010), 80–81.

4. David Masci, "Scientists and Belief" under Religion and Science in the United States, November 5, 2009, https://www.pewresearch.org/religion/2009/11/05/scientists-and-belief/

### *Chapter 1*

1. Steve Rosenberg, "Putin gathers allies to show West's pressure isn't working," BBC, 23 October 2024, https://www.bbc.com/news/articles/cly3ylwg4eqo

### *Chapter 3*

1. John 8:12
2. Hebrews 3 and 4
3. "How Accurate Is Carbon Dating?," Labmate Online, May 20, 2024, https://www.labmate-online.com/news/news-and-views/5/breaking-news/how-accurate-is-carbon-dating/30144
4. Jonathan O'Callaghan, "What Is Time?" in *How It Works* magazine, last updated August 26, 2022, https://www.space.com/time-how-it-works
5. "How Do Planets Form?" https://science.nasa.gov/exoplanets/how-do-planets-form/
6. Aleisha Johnson, "Ode to Oxygen," Ask an Earth and Space Scientist at Arizona State University, https://askanearthspacescientist.asu.edu/explore/early-atmosphere

### *Chapter 4*

1. Revelation 12:4
2. Genesis 3:8
3. Job 1:7–12
4. Genesis 3:8
5. Genesis 4:1–8

### *Chapter 5*

1. Genesis 4:20–22

2. Kay Smythe, "Archaeological Discoveries Are Rewriting What We Know of Neanderthals," *The Daily Caller*, 8/21/24, https://dailycaller.com/2024/08/21/archaeology-neanderthal-monster-beast-pyrenees-spain-intelligent/

3. Ibid.

4. Genesis 4:26

5. Dr. Rick Potts, "Human Origins: What Does It Mean to Be Human?," Smithsonian National Museum of Natural History, https://www.naturalhistory.si.edu/education/school-programs/grades-6-12/human-origins-what-does-it-mean-be-human

6. Job 1

7. Revelation 12:4

8. Hebrews 4

### *Chapter 6*

1. Genesis 2:17

2. Ephesians 1:3–10

3. Matthew 9:27–30

4. Ephesians 1:3–10

5. Job 1

6. 1 John 5:18

7. Matthew 11:15; Mark 4:9; Revelation 2: 7, 11, 17

8. Ephesians 2:8

9. 1 Corinthians 13:13

10. Philippians 4:13

### *Chapter 7*

1. Matthew 27: 51–54

2. Shuang Liu, Yan Wang, Ziyi Ma, Chris Qihan Zou, and Lihuan Zhou, "China's International Climate-Related Finance Provision and Mobilization for South-South Cooperation," World Resources Institute, September 16, 2024, https://www.wri.org/

research/chinas-international-climate-related-finance-provision-and-mobilization-south

3. House Foreign Affairs Committee, "Chinese Communist Party (CCP) Threat to American Universities," https://foreignaffairs.house.gov/wp-content/uploads/2020/02/CCP-Threat-of-American-Universities-V3.pdf

4. Julia Simon, "China is building six times more new coal plants than other countries, report finds," NPR: March 2, 2023, https://www.wqln.org/npr-news/npr-news/2023-03-02/china-is-building-six-times-more-new-coal-plants-than-other-countries-report-finds

***Chapter 8***

1. Alexis de Tocqueville, *Democracy in America*, Part I, Translator? Publisher, Year, Page number

2. Editorial Board of *Nine Commentaries on the Communist Party*, *How the Specter of Communism Is Ruling Our World*, The Epoch Times, 2020), xviii.

3. Ryszard Legutko, *The Demon in Democracy: Totalitarian Temptation in Free Societies* (NY: Encounter Books, 2016), 5-6.

4. Fact Sheet: *Fathers Matter – Pass It On*, Center for Opportunity Now at America First Policy Institute, June 24, 2024, https://www.americafirstpolicy.com/issues/fact-sheet-fathers-matter-pass-it-on

5. Dr. Alveda King and Jack Brewer, "This Black History Month let's shine a spotlight on fatherlessness and saving Black babies," America First Policy Institute February 1, 2023, https://www.foxnews.com/opinion/black-history-month-shine-spotlight-fatherlessness-saving-black-babies

6. Welfare Budget, https://federalsafetynet.com/welfare-budget/

7. Harrell W. Chesson et. al, "The Estimated Direct Lifetime Medical Costs of Sexually Transmitted Infections Acquired in the United States in 2018," National Library of Medicine, November 28, 2023, https://pmc.ncbi.nlm.nih.gov/articles/PMC10684254/

8. Jessica Miller, "Porn Addiction Statistics, " AddictionHelp .com, last updated January 17, 2025 https://www.addictionhelp .com/porn/statistics/

9. Naomi Brower, "Effects of Pornography on Relationships," Utah State University Extension, revised April 2023https:// extension.usu.edu/relationships/research/effects-of-pornography -on-relationships

10. Maria Baer, "More Christians Are Watching Porn, But Fewer Think It's a Problem," *Christianity Today*, September 26, 2024, https://www.christianitytoday.com/2024/09/pornography -use-christians-study-barna-research-pure-desire-ministries/

11. Felix Richter, "60% of Porn Websites Are Hosted in the United States," Statistica.com, August 21, 2013, https://www .statista.com/chart/1383/top-10-adult-website-host-countries/

12. "Fact Sheet: 77 Percent of American Youth Can't Qualify for Military Service," Council for a Strong America, January 24, 2023, trongnation.org/articles/2006-77-percent-of-american-youth -can-t-qualify-for-military-service

The theological elements from
*What the Bible Really Says*
play out in life in Senator DeMint's novel

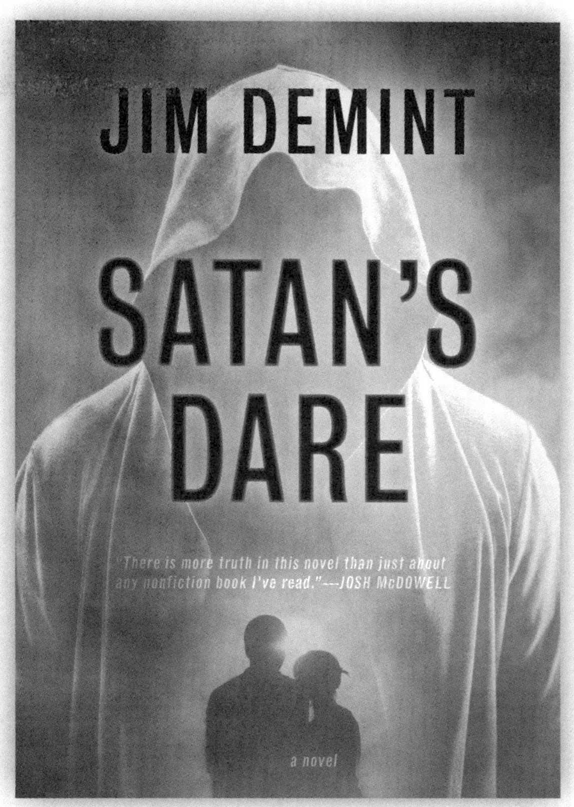


*Satan's Dare: A Novel*
9781735856308 HC / 9781735856315 eBook